THE COMPLETE GUIDE TO

PASTORAL LEADERSHIP

A compendium of essential knowledge,
research and experience for all
pastoral leaders in schools

AMY-MAY FORRESTER

First published 2022

by John Catt Educational Ltd,
15 Riduna Park, Station Road,
Melton, Woodbridge IP12 1QT

Tel: +44 (0) 1394 389850
Fax: +44 (0) 1394 386893
Email: enquiries@johncatt.com
Website: www.johncatt.com

ISBN: 978 1 915261 04 5

Set and designed by John Catt Educational Limited

CONTENTS

CHAPTER 1
AN INTRODUCTION

Pastoral care.

Two words that we hear a lot in schools.

But what do they mean? The history of pastoral care, and its subsequent rise in schools, is an interesting tale of just how far education – and pastoral care provision in schools – has come in a relatively short space of time.

It would be unheard of now for a school not to 'do' pastoral care. One thing we can all agree on, I would hope, is just how important it is. There is an acknowledgement that the wellbeing and development of children must form an integral part of education if children are to thrive.

Schools are a universal service open to every young person. They are also therefore one of the key universal services that form the front line for safeguarding children and ensuring that their needs are met in the right way.

It hasn't always been this way. When we trace its origins, we can see that the idea of pastoral care as we know it today was introduced in the late 1970s by head teacher Michael Marland. Marland wrote a number of books that focussed on schools and classrooms. He went on to be the founding chair of NAPCE, the National Association for Pastoral Care in Education. His book *Pastoral Care*, published in 1974, marks a shift in culture that continues to develop to this day. Pastoral care is now firmly cemented in the heart of schools. Those of us that work within it know first hand just how much it matters to the success children experience in school, whether that be academically, socially, or personally.

As the role of pastoral care has become embedded and developed over time, so too have the demands. Increasingly, services are under more and more demand, and the role schools play in this cannot be underestimated. The role of a pastoral leader is increasingly outward facing, working with other agencies and providing help and support to keep children and their communities safe. It has become one of the most important roles in the safeguarding and welfare of students.

A lot of this care and support happens behind the scenes. The vast majority of school staff will be unaware of it. They know it happens, but the extent to which is happens and the regularity with which it happens are so often unseen.

Despite all the challenges pastoral care throws our way, I truly believe that it is the very best job to have in a school. It is frantic, demanding, emotional, hard, joyful and heartbreaking, often in the same hour! There's no job quite like it.

The people working in pastoral care, though – they really are something special. I've met so many incredible professionals doing life-changing work in the hardest of circumstances. It takes a certain type of person to work in pastoral care. I call it our 'pastoral bones'. It's certainly not for everyone – and nor should it be. That said, I do firmly believe that everyone who works in a school should get some practical experience in it. The level of understanding and perspective that it gives you, and the insight into the challenges your students and your community face, really do change you as a professional.

If you're reading this book as someone interested in getting into pastoral work, seize the opportunity to get some hands-on, voluntary experience. I guarantee it'll be the best thing you ever do. You'll fall in love with this thing we call pastoral care.

Reading this book

The purpose of this book is not to teach anyone to suck eggs. It is designed to cover all the key research and academic content that you need to know as a pastoral leader, with accompanying practical advice and suggestions, sharing real, on-the-ground advice that I have picked up along the way. Each chapter also has summaries of the content in Key Learning Points, alongside a short opportunity for you to apply your learning from each chapter.

There are a great many books for pastoral staff, but there wasn't one that I felt combined the academic knowledge with practical, real-world experience, and which helped to bridge the gap between theory and practice. Each chapter also contains recommended reading – the books that are excellent examples of developing our knowledge and expertise in a range of different areas that can impact and influence our practice in a positive way. They are the 'must reads'. In short, this book seeks to be a hybrid – it will cover research and evidence that all pastoral leaders should know about, alongside real-world examples of operational pastoral care, and help you begin to apply it in practice. I can't claim to have all the answers; no one *ever* does in pastoral care. But I hope that this book gives you some food for thought and support along the way in the best job that exists in a school.

REFERENCES

Marland, M. (1974). *Pastoral Care: Organizing the care and guidance of the individual pupil in a comprehensive school.* London: Heinemann Educational.

CHAPTER 2
VISIONS, STANDARDS, AND HIGH EXPECTATIONS

In pastoral care – much like in the wider school – vision, standards, and high expectations are vital to your success as a leader. However, all too often, when you're appointed to a pastoral role, you may have had very little experience of this. Don't let this put you off – there is always something to learn on the job as a pastoral leader, whether you are five days or five years into your role.

You've run the classroom as a classroom teacher; now you're running the year group.

It feels like a significant step up, both in terms of responsibility and in terms of the scale of the task at hand. It is not uncommon to have between 200 and 400 students in your charge as a pastoral leader. This can, obviously, feel overwhelming, especially if you have not had any form of pastoral responsibility before.

I remember when I first stepped into the role and those far more experienced than me would tell me that it's just like running and leading a classroom. I also remember being told to talk about classroom leadership at pastoral interviews, as though it was the most obvious thing in the world. I couldn't see it then – and I think it is only with the benefit of hindsight and experience that you begin to see this. Once this clicked in my head, creating an aspirational vision became easier. Getting there, though, took time! If I think back to my first years of pastoral work, my focus was on reacting: reacting to students; reacting to events; reacting to the calendar. Reacting, reacting, reacting. And a bit of panicking thrown in for good measure. I wasn't even spinning the plates; they were spinning me.

What I hadn't grasped was that pastoral care needs to be front loaded – you are the architect of your year group, the captain of the ship. Much in the same way that classroom management works, there needs to be a clear vision at the heart of pastoral leadership. You craft, build, and refine the culture in your year group.

And, unfortunately, this is where you can become stuck – too often, teachers are submersed in fluffy, unclear 'visions' of what we are aspiring to. If you don't have a clear, concrete vision of how you want things to run, to achieve your aims for young people, it becomes impossible to create it.

A wise person once told me that if you can see it, you can build it. They weren't wrong. But this is hard, especially at first, and especially if it is a role that you are new to. Your expectations are all over the place – especially if you're in a school that might have had weaker pastoral leadership previously, or if your standards are more demanding than students may have been used to previously.

In the same way that in a classroom you consider the specific behaviours and routines of your class, you need to do the same for your year group. It is important to identify all the opportunities for doing so, from what happens when students enter in the morning, to how you want them to find you, to the ways in which they speak to you and to others. Everything that encompasses specific behaviours also encompasses culture. Culture is built through teaching, modelling, and refining those specific, concrete behaviours until they become habit.

Rather than considering fluffy and meaningless inspiring visions, consider the following:

- What behaviours and attitudes do your students need to develop to be equipped to be successful learners?
- What atmosphere do you want for your year group?
- What do you want to be their daily norm?

- What systems do you need in place to ensure all students can access support?
- What do you want students to learn in their pastoral curriculum time?
- What provision do you need in place to help grow them into excellent young adults?
- What important milestones are there in your time together, and what knowledge do they need – and when – to excel in these?

These are the nuts and bolts of pastoral care: pastoral care is about creating cultures in which all young people thrive. Where people often go wrong lies in thinking the role is all about problems – that's certainly part of it, but it needs to be a thread woven into a wider, clear culture where students thrive. For young people, if they are not thriving personally, they sure as hell won't thrive academically. And that's why we are all here after all: to educate the next generation; to give them new and exciting opportunities in life; to ensure that they are safe. This is where you make the difference as a pastoral leader.

In my first year of teaching, I worked in a school whose motto was 'changing lives through learning'. At the time, I didn't really understand how fundamentally important this is. Learning really does have the power to change lives for the better – and the role of a pastoral leader/head of year is to clear the path for this to happen, to operate in the background, keeping the wheels turning as the driving force of changing lives. Whilst there will be many welfare demands on your time, it is important to keep this at the heart of what we do. Students come to school to learn, to experience the joy and wonder of an ambitious and demanding curriculum, to experience things that they cannot experience at home, and to achieve things that they never thought were possible. Keep this in sight in all that you do.

It's easy to buy into this as an ideal. No one gets into teaching, or indeed pastoral work, because they don't want to give young people the best start in life. Just because we buy into it, doesn't, unfortunately, make it easy. This is the truism of pastoral care. Our role is so closely tied in with supporting young people, often through the very worst that life has viciously thrown at them. We become invested in them in ways that non-pastoral staff often don't realise. We're their cheerleader, their confidante, their school mam, their biggest fan, their stern aunty. This can bring a whole new challenge to holding your expectations high. When you know the trauma children have experienced, when you see the raw emotional pain etched on their faces, it can be easy to think that cutting kids a bit of slack is a kindness.

After all, they've had a really difficult time, haven't they? They've 'got a lot going on'. We need to go easy on them. What can we expect?

What can we expect from kids *like that*?

I hope you have read that last sentence in the spirit in which it was intended – to highlight what we really mean when we look to excuse young people because of their circumstances.

What we are, in effect, saying, is that we don't think they can do it; we don't think they're capable of being and doing better; we don't have faith in them … we're prepared to stand by and let them fail. And this, fundamentally, is where the wheels can come cascading off in pastoral care, because our hearts are fickle beasts. They trick us into thinking it is a kindness to lower expectations. It isn't.

In what feels like compassion, you are in fact letting students down. Keeping your expectations sky high is the real kindness here; that is how pastoral leaders change lives. You are instilling the belief in your students that life's adversities are not something to be feared, that they're not something that has to ruin their chances. Of course, that is not to say that they come without difficulty or challenge – quite the opposite. This is vital for our young people – they grow into adults who can face adversity with resilience and tenacity. Not only can they face it, but they can also navigate their way through it; they've done it before. They've persevered through their difficulties and continued to thrive. They've experienced challenges and survived them. They have the strength of character, and the successful track record, to draw on their developing resilience and take on the challenges that life throws at all of us at one time or another. Giving the gifts of resilience and stoicism, but also determination and hope, is just about the best we can do as pastoral leaders.

One of the hardest parts of this, truly – and I wouldn't be human if I didn't say I hadn't felt this at times too – is to say that having those expectations and holding the line can be difficult sometimes. It can feel harsh or unkind. It can feel like you're being too hard on students. But honestly, and speaking from bitter experience, this is where a truly excellent pastoral care system should kick in. We cannot have these expectations if we aren't also going to ensure that students are adequately and appropriately supported to help them meet our expectations. That's the world that pastoral care needs to live in: to do all that we can to ensure every student can meet our expectations. We ensure that we develop systems and cultures where you can have your expectations *because* you have an excellent pastoral system wrapping itself around the young people in your care.

All too often, though, well-meaning but ultimately disastrous practices emerge. From students leaving lessons left, right, and centre to 'have a chat', through to seeking out pastoral staff to excuse them from sanctions, to having a cup of tea and a biscuit after telling a teacher to 'fuck off', pastoral care in a school can go seriously awry and risk undermining an entire school's efforts. If you ever find yourself with one of your more challenging characters telling staff that they're off to see you to get you to, effectively, undermine them by removing sanctions or overruling them, you've gone horribly, horribly wrong. Equally, if you're working in a system where this is the norm, politely and professionally challenge it. It is only through professional discussion and debate that these ideas can be identified as what they are: well-meaning but misguided attempts to bandage over the cracks of a malfunctioning school.

The simple truth of the matter is that the pastoral system is the beating heart of any school, and it needs to be treated as such. You wouldn't want a weakened heart trying and failing to pump blood to your brain; you'd want strength and power. This is the same for the pastoral system. We set the tone and we build the culture. Classroom teachers ultimately rely on the pastoral system far more than pastoral leaders often realise, especially non-teaching pastoral leaders. If the system is weak and students can leave lessons willy-nilly or seek out a brew and cosy chat in place of a sanction, they're doomed from the start. If students perceive you as someone that will overrule their teachers, or who will backtrack on a sanction if they're difficult enough about it, you aren't doing anyone any favours. You're creating a system whereby teachers cannot have high expectations, because you undermine their attempts. All too often, pastoral and academic are 'at loggerheads', with what often feels like different priorities. This is a danger sign that something is going very wrong. Ultimately, this disparity and disagreement weakens any school. Teachers are here to teach. Children are here to learn. A pastoral system must fundamentally be built with this in mind. Its purpose is to ensure that students are in lessons, are learning, and are supported to attend school. We are not there to undermine the academic priorities of classroom teachers.

Designing your vision

To get where you want to be, you need to spend some time designing your year group. By design, I mean running through exactly and precisely how you want things to operate. Once you know the desired outcome, you then look at achieving that operationally. Achieving operational outcomes is the most important part of this; this is where you build your culture. Your actions become your culture.

Example

Goal: I want form time to be highly structured and purposeful.

Operations to achieve this:

- Fully resourced pastoral programme
- Clear rules in place in form time (what are these rules and why do I want them?)
- Communication of rules (how will students and staff know and enforce these?)
- Maintaining and enforcing rules (how will tutors achieve consistency in their enforcing of the rules?)
- What will I do to check whether form time is highly structured and purposeful?

Depending on your school systems, you might also want to think about other key areas of the students' day where you have ownership and accountability for their conduct:

- What social norms do I want to create when students arrive at school?
- What will break times look like?

- What will lunch times look like?
- How do I want my year group to deal with problems as they arise during the day?
- What impression do you want parents to have of you?
- What routines do I need to have for students?

Overcommunication

We've established already that high expectations can feel difficult to implement sometimes, but it cannot be overstated just how important they are. They will underpin everything that you do, as well as making your job a lot easier in the long run – prevention is better than cure.

To be able to do this, it's important that you have done the groundwork as a pastoral leader. Much as a head of department needs to bring their team with them, you need to bring yours with you – they're just younger!

This means your students knowing exactly what your culture is well before you need to rely on it. This is where my favourite strategy of overcommunication comes in. Every communication you have with students, parents, staff, and governors is an opportunity to reinforce your culture, aims, and ideals, as well as to normalise those behaviours that you want to see as routine everyday experiences.

Spend some time identifying what opportunities you have for reinforcing this. For example: speaking to a child about their behaviour; writing a letter to parents about key events in the year. There will be loads. Then, think about what key ideas you want to reinforce each time – thread this together into a year, and work out every opportunity you have, so that your ethos becomes so routine and predictable that it becomes business as usual. My personal favourite that I endeavour to get into every communication is the idea that when you let a child off you let them down. Many a child has repeated this back to me, eyes rolling but with a delightfully cheeky smirk; they know what they're getting before it even happens. This strategy of overcommunication does so much leg work for you.

Architecture of expectations and routines

Just as construction is a key part of bringing your architecture to life, so constructing and reinforcing your pastoral culture is key. If you're a teaching head of year, think of this in the same way that you think of classroom routines. In the classroom, a teacher will have routines for a myriad of things, and you need the same in pastoral care. But the key here is in how you choose them – they need to be enforceable. In too many schools, rules are set with no realistic chance of successfully implementing them or challenging their value. In turn, this creates a culture in a school that says to students that you don't care about the rules; you can't enforce them. They're pretend rules. Having any of these within your pastoral system will only serve to weaken it further. You don't want to be the head of year who has rules they can't enforce. Not only does it weaken how you are perceived as the leader of the year group, but it chips away at whole school culture too.

As a pastoral leader, there was a standout moment for me where this crystalised in my head. I picked up a year group in year 10 and they were entirely unknown to me. I hadn't taught them, and I hadn't worked with them at any stage. The way we ran lunch times in my school was that students would line up in form groups before being dismissed into lunch. However, not knowing students' names and faces meant that this could not be enforced with any consistency or certainty. The very last thing that I wanted to show my year group was that there was a weakness in chain. Instead, we moved to line up 30 students that could be made up of peer groups rather than forms. This meant that it was entirely possible to enforce, reinforce, and sanction as an expectation. We avoided creating a rule that we say is a rule but really isn't a rule at all. Now, having had this experience, this is one of the first things that I check for if we are making changes within school, or in terms of the rules we already have. The important part of this is that it is the certainty of a sanction, when a rule is broken, that matters. This is what influences students' behaviour choices.

To a certain extent, the vast majority of rules in schools are whole school. Where they are not something that can be enforced consistently, part of your role is to discuss that with your leadership team. Generally, people will tend to believe that something is working unless they are specifically told that it is not. It is those in key operational roles, such as pastoral leaders, who are often best placed to measure this, and, crucially, to feed back when something needs tweaking or changing. In some areas, this can be sufficient, but there is always room for creating your own pastoral rules to contribute to your culture. For example, this can be as simple as lining up in single file, facing the front, at lunch time. Whatever it is, the important thing is that it can consistently be enforced. The reasons for this are twofold: you've selected routines that positively contribute something to your culture, but that also show you can, and will, enforce them. It's that delicate balancing act that any excellent pastoral leader seems to embody – being approachable and positive whilst also being able to strike the fear of God into them if they've let you down.

Assemblies

Assemblies are a significant cog in the wheel of both your school and your pastoral culture. They serve a multitude of purposes, from sharing important information, to raising the profile of important topics, to improving behaviour, to ensuring key messages are also picked up by staff. They are a prime opportunity to build and shape your culture. Assemblies also need to be both proactive and reactive; there will be time where you need to react to events in the world, in your community, in your year group. There's a danger, as always in pastoral care, that you become entirely reactive and miss out anything proactive.

You should have a plan for the year/key stage that outlines the important dates within their learning journey; think options, exams, post 16 applications. Put these in your plan first; you will need to address these. Following that, look for national/international events such as Pride Month, Black History Month. It's important that you ensure that every child feels their culture and diversity are recognised and celebrated in your school. Your calendar will soon fill up, helping you to see that if you factor in some reactive time you're left with very little time for proactive work. That must be your priority; assembly contact with students is a significant part of the puzzle when it comes to crafting your culture. It is your chance to stand in front of a year group as a role model, to challenge them, to inspire them, to educate them; the list is endless.

It took me a long while to see the importance of this and really understand it, especially when new to giving assemblies. My priority then was coming up with enough content to talk for ten minutes without drying up – in many ways, when you're new to pastoral care, it's like being a newly qualified teacher in so many respects. Don't let this put you off – preparation is key here. In my early days, I would write my entire assembly out word for word, not necessarily to read from it verbatim, but to make sure I knew what I would be saying at each point. Much as lesson planning takes an eternity when you're new in the classroom, the same is true of assemblies. But do take some solace in the fact that it becomes significantly quicker the more you do it, exactly as it does with classroom teaching. Before you know it, you'll be preparing it in your head in much less time. Remember too that your audience is not just your year group, but also your tutor team. There are important messages that can be delivered via this medium that also serve a purpose in communicating your vision with your team. Assemblies are an extra opportunity for CPD for staff – think about how your key messages support whole school focusses and give direction as to how students are part of any drive for improvement in a school.

Case study – applying expectations

Ellen is head of year 9, and she will be taking her year group through to the end of year 11. By the October half term, her year group are pushing boundaries. They are not lining up for lunch properly. In September, she had told them to line up in forms. She found this difficult to enforce because the year group were new to her. She didn't know which forms they were in and had to trust them to do as she'd asked. It's now becoming clear to her that they aren't lined up in forms. She's struggling to challenge it because she's accepted it as acceptable behaviour for twelve school weeks already.

Alongside this, her students are increasingly leaving their lessons and arriving at her door, especially if something has gone wrong in lessons. Her office is close to a lot of their lessons, so both staff and students see it as a convenience. Other times, students roam the school looking for her. This averages four to six students per day – she's spending her day firefighting. Just as she's put out one fire, another arrives at her door. By the time lunch time rolls around, she's too tired to fight the line-up battle.

Students are also now beginning to challenge other rules. Their use of language in the corridor is increasingly inappropriate. She regularly hears swear words as students pass her office. She can't always be sure who it is, so she doesn't react to it. Alongside this, there is an increasing trend of behaviour deteriorating in lessons. Students are testing, pushing, and destroying boundaries. If they are disciplined in lessons for this, they walk out and find her. She can't keep up with this, let alone do the work she'd like to do: supporting students' mental health; engaging with external agencies to get bespoke support for those who need it; praising and rewarding those students who are getting it right.

How can Ellen take back control?

When culture is taking a nosedive, it is important to see the wood from the trees. This can be somewhat of a challenge when you're lost in the wood. It's important to think, question, and reflect. The aim is to pinpoint two things: some quick wins and some longer-term cultural improvements you want to make.

Here, Ellen should be considering: What expectations can I realistically enforce, maintain, and sanction quickly? How do I get some semblance of control back?

Consider where you feel she has gone wrong – and it was early days. She set up a rule in September that she couldn't enforce – lining up in form groups. It might seem inconsequential, but what happened there was inevitable; students learnt that the school had rules, but that they weren't enforced. This in turn can create cultures in which there are regular occurrences of rule breaking without consequence. This gives students the impression that rule breaking doesn't have consequences. Of course, this becomes further complicated when some rules do have consequences and others don't. Confused students, or those with a penchant for teenage rebellion, can find it hard to behave in appropriate ways in this case. It isn't clear how they're expected to behave. This then impacts your culture – and you can see where it is escalating to.

Solution 1: Here, I would suggest an entire reset around the lunch lines – make it one that can be enforced, maintained, and sanctioned easily. The fundamental key to any rule in a school is that it is entirely enforceable; otherwise you are, to all intents and purposes, creating a sub-rule that signals that certain rules don't actually apply. There is nothing more damaging to a school culture than weakness such as this. Moving to something simple that can be enforced would start to correct this weakness. This would put

Ellen in the position of elevated authority, with clear-cut rules that she can enforce every day. It also gives her the opportunity to reward students for correct behaviour, by sending those that are meeting expectations in the best way to lunch first, as well as being in and around her year group in a more positive culture. In resetting one routine, devoting some time to considering where else she can re-establish control would help her turn the tide and change the culture.

Key Learning Point: When creating rules and expectations in your year group, never create a rule that you cannot always enforce.

Solution 2: The next priority must be focussing on those students who are not in the lessons when they should be. It is best in this case to go what I would call 'zero tolerance' on it. For things like this to work, it's important to share this with the leadership team in school. It may be that this is not just a problem within this year group, and a whole school response is required. Equally, it may not, and a more bespoke set of actions for this year group would be the most appropriate way forward. If that is the case, a good place to start is with a reset, and communicating clearly and regularly that this is not a permitted behaviour. Inform students and staff that anyone doing this will be sanctioned. As soon as someone does it, issue the sanction and return them to the lesson. This will take the support of teaching staff, and Ellen needs to consider how to get them on side to help nip this in the bud. Some staff may not see an issue with it – others may even find it beneficial if the student is disruptive or difficult to manage. She needs to find a buy-in. The one thing that unites teachers is learning. Make it clear to both staff and students that missing out on learning is not acceptable. Every minute matters when it comes to learning and every child deserves a school that ensures they have this. If students' behaviour is preventing learning, that should be getting picked up by a whole school system, removing students from lessons to somewhere where they cannot continue to ruin the life chances of others through their own poor choices. If your school doesn't have this, in all honesty, find one that does and thank me later.

Key Learning Point: If you need to make a cultural change, work with your wider school body. Culture is only changed by group action, or as is too often the case, group inaction.

Solution 3: There's a wider cultural shift taking place – not all of this is on Ellen. After all, she's just one pastoral leader, but she's not the only pastoral leader. She's also not the only member of staff in the school. The same is true of you.

Culture and expectations are a whole school issue. This is exactly the kind of issue that should be fed back into the system to your line manager. They will have a wider overview – is this problem unique to this year group, or is it a wider issue? It may be that there's a need for a whole school drive on language use, creating systems for the monitoring and sanctioning of this behaviour, as well as clear boundaries for staff to implement. In this case, Ellen's role is to back staff whenever they sanction students, and to have difficult conversations on their behalf if parents complain to her.

Key Learning Point: You can't fight all the battles. This is a hard thing to balance in pastoral care, but it's a vital one. In a demanding, intense role such as this, you must know where to channel your energies and where to draw the line. This is where effective line management comes in. Line management of pastoral care can make or break you – there's such a thing as delegating up, and issues like this are exactly that. Really effective line management helps you to develop your role in the wider school system, both in delegating upwards but also in doing your role effectively to support the wider aims of the school. It was only when I was line managed by an incredible senior leader, Dr Michelle Henley, that I learnt the power of where the middle and senior leadership sweet spot is. The overlap is where the good stuff happens; it's where you feed into the wider school improvement and play your part in securing a whole school improvement.

What you could do to avoid becoming Ellen

Ahead of a new academic year, dedicate a chunk of time to working out what your rules and expectations will be regarding students' conduct. It's useful to do this alongside looking over the calendar for the first half term and working out what things you need to plan and aim for, and what time you have available. That first half term is golden time for setting expectations – you should have a plan for how you will do this over those weeks in school.

The art of building a culture, in truth, isn't down to the severity of the expectation or rule, it's about creating the illusion of boundaries that are enforced, leading to a culture within a school where it's clear that there are authority figures, and that the school is in control of the culture within it. Often people think that authority is a bad thing, as though it is a bad thing for children to experience. I would argue the opposite; it creates environments where children know that the adults are in control. They feel safe and secure in their learning environment. Children need to feel safe and secure in school if they are going to thrive in their learning and development. There are far too many schools, still, where children don't feel safe. No pastoral leader ever wants a child to feel this way, but creating this safe learning environment is a team effort in which you play an important role – of all the people in the building, you know just how much this matters to young people.

RECOMMENDED READING

Some of the key works of literature in relation to pastoral care are those written about school culture and leadership. Whilst they may seem unrelated to your role, they're not. Your year group is a school within a school: you are responsible for leading and managing a team of staff (form tutors); you will lead a team of external agencies; you are responsible for students' provision; you're leading on key moments in the academic year and in their lives. Leadership texts apply to you in all the same ways. Reading widely about culture and leadership couldn't be more important within pastoral care. In most schools, you're leading a team of hundreds of teenagers – you need to be at the top of your game! With this in mind, I have listed here some of the texts that have had the biggest impact on my development and thinking. Not only is it important to our leadership development, but this immersion in thinking about the leadership of schools is a formative part of your development as a pastoral leader. Whilst it may be a busy, demanding job, keeping up to date, reading around topics, and challenging your thinking are a key part of how you'll develop. Too often, we associate subject leadership with reading and thinking, and pastoral leadership with doing. We'd be wrong to see it that way – embody your inner geek and read, read, read.

Handscome, J. (2021). *A School Built on Ethos: Ideas, assemblies and hard-won wisdom.* First edition. Carmarthen: Crown House Publishing.

In this book, Handscombe provides inspiration for how assemblies can contribute beautifully to a whole ethos. Assemblies are often a neglected part of our development, but also a neglected part of the role that we talk about. Partly because they can be deeply personal, and partly because they differ so much between staff and schools, it can be hard to pin down what makes excellent assemblies. Handscombe does an excellent job in this book of changing the dialogue around assemblies. The more we can read, share, and view, the better we will become in this vital aspect of our job.

Birbalsingh, K. (2020). *Michaela: The Power of Culture: The Michaela Way.* First edition. Woodbridge: John Catt Educational.

The second in a series of books exploring the significant successes at the inner London school Michaela Community School, Birbalsingh and her staff explore a range of their philosophies and how they have translated these into a school that is now in the top 10 schools nationwide for progress, alongside securing exceptional outcomes for disadvantaged young people. A controversial read, there may be bits that you differ from ideologically, but that isn't what this book is about – it is a masterclass in creating a culture that you want. Again, treat your year group like a school of your own – and learn a thing or two about creating a culture from Birbalsingh and her dedicated and talented staff.

Bennett, T. (2017). *Creating a Culture: How school leaders can optimise behaviour.* Available at: https://assets.publishing.service.gov.uk/government/uploads/system/uploads/attachment_data/file/602487/Tom_Bennett_Independent_Review_of_Behaviour_in_Schools.pdf.

Bennett, the DfE's behaviour tsar, conducted an in-depth review of schools where behaviour was truly exceptional. Whilst the prime focus of the report is behaviour, there remains a lot to be learnt from this in terms of creating a culture within a year group. One key concept that emerges from this report is the phrase 'the way we do things here'. In some schools, this will be a clearly established norm. If you're working in one of these, your year group mission is to support this through your approaches. However, too many of us work in schools where this is not the case, and this makes creating your culture even more of a challenge. Regardless of your context, Bennett's finding is that 'cultures require deliberate creation' (p. 8) and that you must build a culture with as much detail and clarity as possible, alongside maintaining it. Again, those of you with a classroom teaching background will see the similarities between this and classroom teaching, where building your culture, expectations, and routines is at the heart of excellent learning. Put this at the heart of what you do – and remember why it matters; every child deserves to learn to the best of their ability, in a safe and nurturing environment.

REFERENCES

Bennett, T. (2017). *Creating a Culture: How school leaders can optimise behaviour.* Available at: https://assets.publishing.service.gov.uk/government/uploads/system/uploads/attachment_data/file/602487/Tom_Bennett_Independent_Review_of_Behaviour_in_Schools.pdf.

Birbalsingh, K. (2020). *Michaela: The Power of Culture: The Michaela Way.* First edition. Woodbridge: John Catt Educational.

Handscome, J. (2021). *A School Built on Ethos: Ideas, assemblies and hard-won wisdom.* First edition. Carmarthen: Crown House Publishing.

CHAPTER 3
BEHAVIOUR AND PASTORAL CARE

In any school, behaviour – and the management of it – is the single most important thing to get right. Without excellent behaviour, you cannot have excellent learning. Lives won't change without excellent standards. And those same lives won't thrive and develop where expectations of them are low. We've looked already at how standards and expectations make a significant difference in pastoral care, but behaviour in and of itself is also a hugely significant part of any school culture.

Within this, there is also a strong overlap with pastoral care; in fact, I'd go so far as to suggest that behaviour and pastoral care are inseparable. Where students' lives present significant challenges, or their previous life experiences lead to added challenges, this inevitably spills over into their behaviour. This is part of our students' lives and experiences – and it often leaves an indelible mark on their lives, one we must acknowledge and support. Too often, though, pastoral care becomes somewhat of an excuse generator – to first consider what students are going through and to lower expectations as a result.

In Chapter 2, I touched on how dangerous and pervasive this can be, and that is never truer than when we are considering behaviour. When we look at the highest performing state schools in the country, we also see that they often have one thing in common: clear behaviour systems, which run alongside the unflinching belief that every child is capable of meeting sky-high expectations. Coupled with this, of course, is ensuring that children get the right support so that they can meet those sky-high expectations.

Rather than lowering expectations so that it is 'easier' for students to meet them, the very best schools push every child to be their very best.

Any system that places high expectations on students needs to be very clearly and robustly underpinned by a pastoral system that supports them to achieve this. Without that, we set students up to fail. Therefore, it is without question that pastoral care must overlap with behaviour in schools. So too must the staffing; the best pastoral leaders know their students inside out. They know their families, their histories, their quirks, their motivators, their foibles. They know what gets them out of bed in the morning, they know how to speak to families in a way that means they're heard. They form relationships that are crucial to improving outcomes for their students. They are, quite simply, best placed to play a formative and important role in ensuring that students' behaviour can improve over time.

Whilst the importance of the pastoral system in behaviour is not controversial, the way behaviour is managed and developed in school is. There are strong feelings on all sides of the debate. It's important that pastoral leaders are well versed in these debates as well as forming their own beliefs. Your beliefs are the things that get you out of bed in the morning, they motivate your courage in steadfastly doing your job against pushback, they give you hope after a day where you feel it doesn't exist. Your views really matter – they become your backbone in a lot of ways in pastoral care. Where you have different views and values to the schools you work in, it becomes incredibly difficult to do the best job that you can. Aligning yourself with a school that shares your vision and passion can ignite special things when it comes to pastoral care.

No excuses and zero tolerance

Over recent years, the phrases 'no excuses' and 'zero tolerance' have become somewhat de rigueur – they symbolise a growing understanding in schools that excusing behaviour and having tolerance of poor behaviour lead schools into difficulty. It's hard not to agree with this; after all, if you're not 'no excuses', are you 'some excuses'?

This, for me, is where the debate becomes fierce – those opposing high-expectation systems take this and, possibly wilfully, misunderstand it. 'If a student's parent died, would you really put them in detention for not bringing their tie?' they cry, as though having high expectations turns you into a heartless monster.

This wilful misunderstanding of the behaviour debate is where it becomes polarised. The truth, in reality, is that we'd give the student a tie, but also apply all of the mechanisms for support that we could. They'd be supported and cared for in the worst moments of their lives; of course, no one is going to put them in a detention for not having a tie the day a family member dies. Anyone that would is in the wrong job, frankly. However, this leads us into murkier waters – what about two years down the line, when the same child forgets their tie and fruitfully tells their maths teacher to 'fuck off' because they asked her to pick up her pen?

Of course, there's a context here; there always is. In my career, it has been rare that there is a student with serious behavioural issues where there isn't a complex context. It becomes a reason – a reason that explains why the student is behaving in the way that they are.

Crucially, though, this cannot become an excuse. When it becomes an excuse, we let them down. We are, to all intents and purposes, saying they cannot excel because of the things that have happened in their life. They won't achieve as much as others. They won't go on to do themselves proud.

And this is where the borderline between behaviour and pastoral care can become muddy. It's very, very easy for a pastoral leader to have such a strong, long-lasting relationship with a student that they do start, through no fault of their own, to think in this way.

I know that because I've been guilty of it myself in the past.

This, for me, is one of the single most important things you must be aware of as a pastoral leader. There is no shame in thinking this or getting to a place with a student where you feel there is an excuse for their behaviour – but what really makes the mark of an excellent pastoral leader is to challenge that thinking, in themselves and in others, and seek to push beyond this. There's no shame in asking respected colleagues: 'Am I being too soft?' – but make sure you're asking someone who shares your understanding of what too soft looks like in reality! Make sure that person is also going to be honest with you.

Of course, there are also cases, which you will come across possibly (hopefully!) more frequently in schools, where there isn't a context. A child simply, and wilfully, pushes back against the school, against teachers, against authority. Some will have you believe that there will always be an 'unmet need' – I'd argue they've not met enough teenagers!

These cases can be more frustrating than those where there is a context – at least with a context in which you can feel empathy and sympathy with a child and work hard for them to get the right support in place. The less this is the case, the more frustrating it can feel playing a significant role in supporting the behaviour of a child in this situation.

This is where strong, clear, whole school behaviour systems really excel – these students know where the boundaries are, staff enforce them regularly, and sanctions are applied. This is why systems matter, and why they make such a difference to a school. Bennett (2020) argues in his book *Running the Room* that it is the certainty of the sanction, rather than the severity, that leads to improvements in behaviour because of clear systems in schools. This is absolutely key. Where systems are unclear, and sanctions are applied in a hit and miss manner, students become confused – why is their behaviour OK in science but not in DT? Why can they tell their mate to fuck off in maths, but in English that comes with a removal from lessons? Some will be confused; but some – and if you've met a teenager at any point, you'll know where this is going – will see this as an opportunity to play the system. To test boundaries. To take advantage of teachers not using the system as they should.

This, too, is where pastoral care comes into its own. In schools where clear, consistent systems are in place, your role is in guiding students through school. Where students have a sanction, your role is to back it whilst supporting them in the right ways, and to help them avoid a similar situation in future.

But in schools where there is a more chaotic approach, your role will be infinitely harder, because your role involves navigating the uncharted waters of various expectations, and having to openly admit to students that there isn't consistency in school, and that *yes*, they do find that difficult, but also that *yes*, they do need to have a sanction in one lesson even though they might have avoided this previously.

It doesn't take a genius to see which system is likely to make the best use of its pastoral leaders, nor which one allows students to understand their behaviours and improve them.

In the chaotic world, we're all firefighting – there's little room for proactive, formative support in helping students to improve their behaviour, because too much time is taken up reacting to it.

In the consistent school, pastoral leaders can excel at what they're good at – working with students to help them do better.

If you're working in the former, good luck and find a new school. If you're lucky, your school might be open to change – push for it. Show them this book if you must. Read the various OFSTED reports of schools with these systems; hell, show them the astronomical Progress 8 scores for the top 10 schools in the country, and their exceptional outcomes for the most disadvantaged students, and then look at their behaviour policies and systems. The correlation is undeniable.

If you happen to work in a school where these systems are already in place and well established, you're a lucky soul. Your role here is in supporting this – clear systems rely on every member of staff using them and supporting them. As a pastoral leader in this Mecca, your role is so, so important to the long-term success of systems such as this. You're the first person students will come to, to protest wildly at how they've been awfully disciplined for 'just picking up a pen' (read: and then launching it at their mate four rows behind) and it really isn't fair.

Your role lies in supporting classroom teachers in their implementation. It involves talking to students about what they got wrong – and sometimes in helping them understand what was wrong about their behaviour. A pastoral leader, must, at all times, support classroom teachers in their use of a behaviour system – the most important thing for a pastoral leader is to never, ever undermine a classroom teacher, even where you feel they might have misjudged something. Deal with that privately. That's what professionals do. To a child, your role is to balance their support needs against supporting the member of staff – they must be equal, and one must not outbalance the other. In my experience, where teachers do sometimes get something wrong, which we do, because we are human and fallible, there will be a genuine recognition of that, coupled with a desire to repair a relationship with a student. Your role, as pastoral leader, is to support and facilitate that, and play a role in moving forward in a positive way. Middle leadership of any kind is ultimately about playing your specialist role in ensuring that teachers can teach, and that students can learn. Of course, our role focuses on wellbeing and safeguarding, but so too should it be equally balanced by serving our staff, creating the conditions for them to do what they love to do; teach.

Sanctions and restorative practice

Schools, when you think about it, have precious few weapons at their disposal when it comes to sanctions.

A detention, also known as sitting a room, is hardly a significant deterrent.

An exclusion, also known as being at home. Also hardly a significant deterrent.

Clearly, there's not much of a deterrent in schools. And yet, sometimes the hysteria around sanctions in schools seems to lose sight of what schools are trying to achieve. Some schools, in fact, eschew sanctions entirely and follow an entirely restorative practice. However, I would argue that any functional school needs both. Sanctions work as a deterrent for the vast majority of students – they work in general in society. Think about speeding offences, for example. How often would you speed up on sight of a speed van? Never. Because there is a deterrent, and one that is consistent. The same principle applies to the vast majority of our students – and without those small but significant deterrents, too many students wouldn't know the boundaries of acceptable conduct in schools. Or, they might challenge them more frequently if the consistency is questionable. No one likes being pulled up on something they've not been told off for in the past – of course our reaction may not be the ideal one. The same is true of children. The consistency of the sanction, as outlined in Chapter 2, plays a hugely significant role.

Restorative practice aims to do something different – to prevent relationship-damaging incidents from happening in school and to resolve them where they do. Very few people would argue that there isn't a place in schools for restorative practice. There is, and it is an important part of moving past serious incidents, especially between peers or between teacher and student. However, the danger comes when restorative practice is used as a stand-alone approach, without sanctions at its side. The restorative aspects of the system are often most effective when they incorporate pastoral leaders too.

The vastly different backgrounds of our young people are often overlooked when it comes to behaviour in schools. Whilst different prior knowledge and ability is often talked about and planned for in terms of the academic side of the school, the behavioural side is its much-neglected other half, just as important, but so easily forgotten.

Teachers and academics, those engaged in discussions around teaching and learning, often talk about 'the Matthew Effect' – the adage that the rich get richer while the poor get poorer. The same is true when it comes to lots of things in school – knowledge, vocabulary, and, ultimately, behaviour. Bennett (2020) outlines this in detail, reminding us very clearly that different students have very different prior knowledge of behaviour. Some students will join us in schools having had behaviour taught to them from an early age. They know how to behave in appropriate ways. They can emotionally manage disappointment or being told to do something they don't want to do. They can self-regulate their emotions and their behaviours.

However, for every student with this privileged background, there will also be an equal who has not had this same level of exposure and teaching in their formative years. And the biggest flaw we see in schools lies in neglecting this, overlooking the very significant role that schools, and those working in them, need to play in taking a proactive approach to the explicit teaching and modelling of behaviour.

A behaviour curriculum

In recent years, there has, quite rightly, been an increased focus on curriculum in schools. Whereas once teachers were glorified children's entertainers, with 'fun' and 'a buzz' the central descriptor of excellent teaching, the focus has changed into much more academic, knowledge-based explorations of subjects in all of their rich, powerful beauty. The curriculum is now a celebration of the best that respective subjects have to offer, with both depth and breadth of learning at the heart of what curriculum leaders and classroom teachers do.

This welcome change in schools is already proving what a significant impact a knowledge-rich, academic focus can have, especially on disadvantaged students. However, one thing that is often neglected in schools is the proactive curricular work that can be done on behaviour.

In schools where outcomes and progress are astronomical, where the disadvantage gap has closed, or even exceeded the more privileged, all have this in common: they teach behaviour alongside the academic curriculum. They acknowledge that all students will have a different starting point with their behaviour, and they aim to level the playing field to ensure that all students are equipped with the exact knowledge they need to succeed in their school, both academically and behaviourally. This should be a core focus within the pastoral system; academic curriculum time is often packed and in demand.

However, pastoral teams often have some time at their disposal – registration, PSHE – there are an infinite number of staffing models where pastoral care and the time allocated are wildly different, and rightly so, given that schools should be responsive to their individual context and needs.

As a pastoral leader, some of that time will be at your disposal. An interesting activity to help you explore where your gaps are would be to consider the extent to which your school clearly sets out its behavioural expectations, and then consider what it does to teach behaviour clearly and explicitly to students. If there is a discrepancy between the two, there is a gap to be filled, and the pastoral system can be an excellent part of addressing this, alongside other whole school approaches.

Having done this recently, I was embarrassed to find that precious little time was spent on this. It's one of those things that sounds obvious when you hear it, but up until that point it perhaps wasn't so clear. It's no bad thing to find that your school may be in a similar position. Schools have come a long way with behaviour over the past years, but there are inevitably things that we haven't got quite right yet. That's all part of the wider school improvement journey; no school is the finished article. As a pastoral leader, part of a wider pastoral team, you and your colleagues are best placed to work on this – to level the playing field, to talk regularly about behaviour, and to teach students how to thrive behaviourally. You will, as a pastoral leader, have a unique insight into what your students' behavioural needs are – and again, this will differ hugely between schools and their respective cohorts. But this is something that can really enhance what you're able to achieve as a pastoral leader – and give students the gift of behaviour, something they will take with them as they grow and develop.

The permanent exclusions debate

Not only has the narrative around behaviour systems in schools become polarised, so too has the narrative surrounding exclusions. Again, there are strong feelings on both sides of the debate, with some claiming that exclusions ruin lives and others claiming quite the opposite.

For me, it's quite a simple issue – exclusions should be as few as possible, but as many as necessary for a school to uphold its expectations and values.

No head teacher ever wants to permanently exclude a child. They know it is a life-altering moment for the child. It is never anything other than a sad day for a school when it does happen. The ability to do it, however, should be the right of every head teacher. They are ultimately responsible for the safety and education of all students in their school. If another child threatens the safety of others, presents a real risk to them, or persistently disrupts their right to an education, a head teacher needs to be able to act in the best interests of their school community. The minute we become 'No Exclusions', we actually endanger students and create unnecessary levels of risk in schools, especially regarding keeping children safe in schools.

As a pastoral leader, you will encounter exclusions, unless, of course, you're crazy enough to work in a no-exclusions school. If you do, I wish you all the luck the world. But, if you're anything like me, you would choose to work somewhere that will exclude if you absolutely have to. Within your role, you'll see the impact on children when their peers' behaviour is abusive, harmful, or downright dangerous. Students should never be too scared to come to school or obtain their right to an education, or to have to live in fear. That, in and of itself, is a safeguarding issue – schools must keep children safe, and an inevitable part of this is exclusions where there are such deep and serious concerns about another student's behaviour and the significant harm it can bring to those in the school's care.

Despite knowing that it is the right thing to do, no one ever wants to exclude a child – and it can be particularly hard for pastoral leaders who have likely worked closely with the student and their family to try to avoid exclusions. You will feel a whole spectrum of emotions, often simultaneously. It'll be a strange mixture of sadness, relief, anger – and many others, I'm sure. Whenever you work with a child where a permanent exclusion features, I can guarantee that they will leave an impact on you as a professional. You will learn and develop in all manner of new ways. You'll feel deep frustrations at the dire state of support for young people. You'll be angry that a permanent exclusion is sometimes the best way to get a child the help they need, or a placement in education provision that can best meet their needs. You might even feel a sense of happiness, especially where you know that it is the right thing for the child. It can be odd and strange feeling that – we're taught to demonise exclusions, and having a positive emotion about them might feel a little alien. Don't be surprised by this, or convince yourself that you're broken as a pastoral leader if you do. Sometimes, the knowledge that the child will get what they need will bring you positive emotions; you're no monster for that. Your relationship with that child and their family will be long and, no doubt, complex. These things always affect you. The day they don't is the day you should consider whether this is still the job for you.

Despite the effort, time, and support that you will have no doubt put into working with a student at risk of exclusion, when it comes to a safety issue, your focus and care as a pastoral leader must also be equally focussed on those impacted negatively by another student's behaviour. They matter just as much. Education and learning are precious gifts, and every minute really does matter in a school; it changes lives. We cannot seek to jeopardise that through an ignoble attempt to be 'No Exclusions'.

Practical strategies

Student behaviour plans

To ensure that students who present with challenging behaviour are well supported, it's important that pastoral leaders play a significant role in leading on what that support looks like. Students are individuals and often need a more personalised approach. In putting this together, it should be a collaborative process between you, the student, their family, and the staff who teach and support them regularly.

1. **Spend some time information gathering.** This is the important part – a plan needs to be helpful, but it also needs to be realistic. Spend time with the student, exploring what they find useful. But this should always be checked out for how realistic it can be within the confines of a classroom, or with the workload pressures that teachers face.

2. **Observe the student in different areas.** If there are lessons that are a real area of success, get in and find out what it is that's working. Sharing this more widely will help classroom teachers support the student's needs.

3. **Outline clearly what 'acceptable behaviour' is.** Everyone involved needs to know what the aim is, the student included. Expectations shouldn't be different from those for any other child in the school, and a support plan shouldn't artificially lower expectations for them in comparison with other students. However, breaking things down into steps for success can really help. For example, if the start of a lesson is crucial to the student getting it right from the outset, outline the behaviours they need to show. This could include enter the room and sit in your seat, get your pen and book out, put your bag on the floor, open your book, begin the task on the board. This way, everyone is clear on what success looks like.

4. **Outline what to do when things go wrong.** This is an important thing to plan ahead for, because things often do go wrong, and everyone supporting a child needs to know what to do in these situations. This will often depend on the student in question and should also be informed by any disabilities or special needs the student might have. Reasonable adjustments can and should be used where a student's disability has a direct impact on their behaviour. For example, if a student with autism has a meltdown if something goes wrong, the better way to support that would be for their key worker to support them 1:1 and help them recover. Immediately applying sanctions won't achieve much in this instance. However, for other students, it will. This is where knowledge of the child's needs, disabilities, and strengths plays a vital role in creating a plan that works for everyone involved.

5. **Remind and review.** Things needs to be kept under review, especially to see where any changes or adaptations need to be made. It's also important to remind everyone involved of the plans – especially if there aren't regular issues that will keep them at the forefront of teachers' minds. Teachers' professional lives are incredibly busy, and some staff can be teaching hundreds of children across their timetable. Your role is to try to make things as easy as you can for them to do what you need them to do to best support the child.

6. **Professional curiosity.** As outlined above, making reasonable adjustments is an important part of school provision. However, there may be other areas that the student needs support in, but that they themselves aren't aware of. Again, these aren't excuses, but ensuring that SENDCOs (special educational needs and/or disabilities coordinators) are involved can help reveal things that may help. For example, if a student has a reading age of five, but is regularly exposed in lessons to text they can't read, this difficulty is likely to be a barrier for them. It's unlikely that they'd have the insight themselves about this – schools need to have a certain level of curiosity to find out what a child's daily experience of learning is, and then respond to it to try to help.

Difficult conversations with parents

This is an inevitable part of the job of a pastoral leader, and one that often strikes the most fear into those aspiring or new pastoral leaders. We've all heard the horror stories.

One of the most important parts of managing difficult conversations is to front load them with a relationship. If you know in advance that a student has difficult parents, or the chances of having some difficult conversations in future are quite high, try to first get ahead of this by building a relationship with the family. It's important in your early contacts with the family that you establish some common ground; you all want the best for the child. It's important that they're able to see you in that light.

Whilst this might not take away the difficult conversations, it does make them run more smoothly when that common ground is already established. Talking to someone you already have a working relationship with is much easier than going in blind. If you can establish that you want the best for the child before the point at which you have these conversations, it will help in the long run when you need to draw on this.

It's also important to consider what the family's relationship with school is like; if they're constantly getting negative messages and communications from the school, it won't take long for that relationship to break down. Try to find ways to consolidate this – pastoral leaders being the sole point of contact can really help keep the amount of contact manageable, but also help to ensure that it's well pitched to the family. This regular contact can help build up positive relationships whilst keeping the amount of contact from the school at a level that is manageable rather than at one that may trigger further disengagement.

There will be other times when you know you're headed for a difficult conversation – often these tend to spring up out of nowhere, or a furious parent arrives in reception. In cases like this, if parents are aggressive or antagonistic, remember you can ask them to book in an appointment time. You can ask them to leave if their conduct is unacceptable. No one should have to put up with that kind of behaviour. They don't have the right to be seen immediately, especially if their behaviour is of concern. By delaying the meeting, it will give them an opportunity to calm down and you an opportunity to plan appropriately for the meeting.

Sometimes, though, that same level of emotion is clear in a pre-planned meeting. I've sat in many of these in my time and watched a number of highly skilled colleagues manage these.

One thing they all had in common was letting the parent talk. Let them get everything out. Listen, make notes, show that you're interested in what they're saying. Of course, if it becomes aggressive, or they're swearing at you, you should always address that head on, and warn them that if it continues the meeting will be terminated. Most parents at this point will calm themselves down – again, let them talk. This can be the hardest part, especially where things may be unfounded or inaccurate. But challenging this quickly will almost always lead to an escalation. By letting them talk, you're able to see the scale of what you're dealing with before proceeding.

Once they've talked, take some time to collaboratively agree what their views/concerns are, and then direct the meeting as a joint approach to finding a positive way forward for those concerns. Keep bringing it back to this – that you're all meeting together for the benefit of the child, because you all care about them and want to see them succeed.

There are some general tips that I always share with new or less experienced colleagues:

1. **Take someone in with you** – especially if you have some worries ahead of the meeting. Discuss your approach ahead of the meeting and make sure you're both clear on roles ahead of the meeting.

2. **Take notes.** This is important if there are any further challenges later down the line, or any disagreements about what was discussed. If your school doesn't already have one, use a meeting pro forma in which you're able to make notes on the key areas of discussion, any agreed actions and timescales, and anything further that needs to be done. At the end of the meeting, use this to summarise the meeting with the family, and ask them to sign it to agree that it is an accurate reflection of the meeting. If it isn't, make some changes together so that you're both in agreement. You might also want to consider asking them to confirm if they were happy with the way that the meeting was carried out, and use this as an opportunity to problem-solve. Ask them to sign the notes to confirm this.

3. **Follow up in writing.** This can be done via email or letter. Equally, a copy of the meeting pro forma, if you're able to use one, can ensure that everyone has a record of what happened and what was discussed.

Reinforcing key messages

Reinforcing expectations of behaviour at regular intervals can really help create a narrative that students buy into. Use your assembly times to talk about why your behaviour expectations matter. Use materials and resources that reflect the values that are shown by your behaviour expectations – and make the connections for students. Be explicit about why the behaviours you're expecting from them are also important in the wider world. Do this in person too – every interaction you have with a student, positive and negative, is an opportunity to reinforce and build your school's behaviour culture.

Case study

Tyler is head of year 10. A boy in his year group, Lewis, is presenting several difficulties in classes. His behaviour is often disruptive – sometimes low level but insidious disruptions that threaten the learning of the rest of the class. Where he is challenged on his behaviour, his reaction can be extreme, often resulting in explosive responses to staff. In English, his teacher reports that things are going really well. He is not picking up behaviour points and there are rarely any outbursts. Maths is the opposite: his maths teacher is concerned about his behaviour, especially his reactions when he is challenged on his behaviour. He regularly picks up behaviour points in maths when he is challenged on his behaviour.

Tyler observes him in English, where there are fewer concerns about his behaviour. When watching the lesson, Tyler notices that Lewis doesn't do a great deal. When the rest of the class get to the lesson, they begin the work on the board. Lewis doesn't. After ten minutes, he gets his pen out and scribbles in his book. Eventually, with some cajoling, he writes a sentence; the rest of the class have written about a side of A4.

Tyler then observes Lewis in maths, where there are more concerns about his behaviour. At the start of the lesson, his teacher asks him to get his things out and begin the work. He doesn't. His teacher asks him again, giving him some time to get things right. The teacher then begins teaching maths. Lewis is muttering under his breath, 'I hate maths.' His teacher challenges this. Lewis becomes annoyed. The teacher continues teaching their maths lesson. When the teacher finishes and asks students to complete the question on the board, Lewis doesn't begin the task. He disengages from the lesson entirely. He begins looking around for other people to distract. His teacher notices this, and rather than challenging his disengagement, she spends a few minutes recapping the maths with Lewis whilst the rest of the class get on with their work. He completes the work in question.

What has Tyler learnt?

Tyler has learnt that there are wildly different expectations of Lewis in different subjects. Where are things going wrong? It's easy to see that these different expectations are leading to all manner of problems. Where Tyler thought Lewis was doing well in English, given his behaviour is never an issue, and poorly in maths, the reverse is actually true. In maths, he is making progress in his learning, and being well supported by his teacher. In English, there is an increasing gap between Lewis and his peers. Lewis is learning very little. Whilst it may appear his behaviour is never an issue, it is only that way because there are low expectations on him and staff are not challenging him.

What do you learn from this?

As a pastoral leader, hopefully you're able to see here that we must look behind what the headline information tells us. It's open to bias. You need to have professional curiosity and take an in-depth look yourself. It would be easy, in this case, to plan for the wrong problem – and ultimately all that would happen is that Lewis would have learnt nothing in English all year. It's a significant reminder that behind the data can sit a very different picture, and reading into behaviour points doesn't always give you the full picture of what's actually going on.

What do you do when you find a problem like this?

It's one you'll come across more than you might expect. It's easy, as teachers, to believe that we have high expectations of students at all times – I've never met a teacher who said they had low expectations! But we can sometimes be out of kilter with others, or with our school, without realising it. Of course, one issue may be that his English teacher has taken the path of least resistance; she finds it easier to tolerate his lack of learning as long as he doesn't kick off, whereas his maths teacher doesn't. It may be a confidence issue. It may be that his English teacher has been unsupported in the past; it could be any number of issues. Your role here is to find out what the root of the problem is and to find a positive way forward for both staff and students.

How do I manage this?

Open, honest, but professional conversations are important here. We owe ourselves, in our profession, a certain level of candour when it comes to students' learning. It isn't OK for students to go through their lessons not completing what they should be completing, but you don't have to deal with that in a way that either criticises or embarrasses his teachers.

They'll know deep down that he is not making the progress he should be making. Teachers rarely come to school to actively go out of their way not to teach students, and it is from that understanding that issues such as this need to be kept in mind. The teachers are the ones dealing with him every day. Treat others the way you'd want to be treated, and make sure that his teachers know they have your full support in dealing with him.

What do I focus on first?

One of the first areas to look at is consistency of expectation for Lewis – and consistency of approach with him. Make it clear to all involved what he is expected to do in each lesson. Make sure his teachers are fully aware of what his behaviour can be like, and what to do when he is not getting it right. In most schools, this will be to follow the school behaviour policy. However, you may be in a school that has a less clear system. In this case, you need to create something that is clear, for Lewis and for his teachers, so that there is a line drawn that clearly outlines what is and is not acceptable. Lewis needs to be involved in this and know clearly what the sanctions will be if he does not meet expectations.

Key Learning Points

1. Pastoral care and behaviour have a strong overlap. You play a vital role in each.

2. Proactive work is important when thinking about improving behaviour in schools.

3. Clear systems help everyone in schools.

4. As a pastoral leader, your role encompasses supporting students and supporting staff.

5. You should never overrule or undermine a teacher, or any other colleague involved in supporting a child.

6. Your role is about finding ways to support both student and teacher in holding tight on expectations and ensuring that students' needs are met in the process.

7. Learning matters and learning changes lives; this is why we need to have high expectations of our students.

RECOMMENDED READING

As I've outlined in this chapter, there is a much wider debate around the topic of behaviour. There is a wealth of reading that you could do to explore a lot of the philosophies that sit behind this topic. It's always a fascinating insight into the profession to immerse yourself in such an array of perspectives. Some will reinforce the way that you feel; others may challenge your thinking. It's important to do both, and to interrogate your own views and perspectives. They have such a significant influence on the way we do this job that we owe it to ourselves and others to make sure we are intellectually engaged with the thinking behind the areas we work within. In this section of recommendations, I'm recommending the texts I feel are pivotal in creating excellent behaviour cultures in schools. There will be countless others, but I feel these help you to form a good grounding in the topic.

Bennett, T. (2020). *Running the Room*. Woodbridge: John Catt Educational.

This text is primarily written for classroom teachers. Some of you will be teaching pastoral leaders; others of you will not be. Regardless, this text is helpful. Not only does it touch on classroom management, but a lot of what Bennett writes focusses on the role that schools play in creating excellent behaviour. It is a must read.

Lemov, D. (2015). *Teach Like a Champion 2.0: 62 techniques that put students on the path to college*. San Francisco, CA: Jossey-Bass.

This is another text that may be more familiar to those of you who are teaching pastoral leaders. The story behind Teach Like a Champion (TLAC) is a significant one. Lemov, a US researcher, sought to explore what the very best teachers did to get the best results from students. He looked at schools that had the best progress and outcomes for disadvantaged learners. In doing this, he sought to explore what it was they had in common, and what we could learn from their practice to spread more widely across education. Thus, TLAC was born. Containing a myriad of techniques that the best teachers had in common, this is a useful manual when looking for classroom techniques that might also be helpful when dealing with individual students, despite being aimed at whole classes. For non-teaching pastoral leaders, this will give you a clear insight into classroom management – and it is a really important area to be knowledgeable in to ensure that you're able to have a professional understanding with qualified teachers.

Education Endowment Foundation (2019). *Improving Behaviour in Schools: Guidance report.* Available at: https://educationendowmentfoundation. org.uk/public/files/Publications/Behaviour/EEF_Improving_behaviour_ in_schools_Report.pdf.

The Education Endowment Foundation (EEF) produce evidence informed guidance for schools with the aim of helping schools to use the 'best bets' for the decisions they make about any school improvement areas. Their behaviour report makes a range of interesting recommendations as well as exploring the importance of teaching learning behaviours. A must read for anyone exploring a behaviour curriculum, or anyone working collaboratively with teaching and learning teams with the overlap between behaviour and learning:

Education Endowment Foundation (2019). *Putting Evidence to Work: A school's guide to implementation.* Available at:https:// educationendowmentfoundation.org.uk/public/files/Publications/.

This is a perfect example of where we can, as pastoral leaders, make use of evidence informed support for schools, and know how best to implement things so that they have more chance of being implemented properly and an improvement happening.

REFERENCES

Bennett, T. (2020). *Running the Room.* Woodbridge: John Catt Educational.

Education Endowment Foundation (2019). *Putting Evidence to Work: A school's guide to implementation.* Available at:https:// educationendowmentfoundation.org.uk/public/files/Publications/.

Education Endowment Foundation (2019). *Improving Behaviour in Schools: Guidance report.* Available at: https://educationendowmentfoundation. org.uk/public/files/Publications/Behaviour/EEF_Improving_behaviour_ in_schools_Report.pdf.

Lemov, D. (2015). *Teach Like a Champion 2.0: 62 techniques that put students on the path to college.* San Francisco, CA: Jossey-Bass.

CHAPTER 4

PASTORAL CARE, COGNITIVE SCIENCE, AND BEST PRACTICE FOR LEARNING

Pastoral care is often considered to be solely focussed on wellbeing, mental health, and safeguarding. Of course, these are areas of significance within the pastoral realm. However, there is a growing acceptance that true pastoral care should also focus on supporting the aims of teaching and learning. Real pastoral care seeks to ensure that students are well supported in their learning and go on to achieve excellent outcomes. What greater gift could a school give to a child than a set of GCSE results that opens the doors to the next stages of their growing lives?

To do this effectively, for as many children as possible, pastoral care needs to be at the heart of any school; children learn best when they are happy, safe, and cared for. This is where the pastoral provision in a school is uniquely placed; its primary role is to bring this into fruition whilst also ensuring that appropriate provision is in place to enable students to advance in their academic studies.

There is a delicate balancing act to be had here, as well as effective teamwork between academic middle leaders of curriculum, teaching and learning leaders, and pastoral leads. When working together, with the best outcomes for students in mind, middle and senior leaders can create a symbiotic relationship between these different disciplines, creating the optimal conditions for success in their context – in their school – for their students.

As education has progressed, in recent years there has been a significant shift in the landscape. Where once curriculum and academic focus was somewhat lost in the edutainment of teaching, now we are, rightly, significantly more focussed on an ambitious, knowledge-rich curriculum, equipping all students, regardless of background or life circumstance, with the same access to the very best that has been thought and said. A new era has dawned, one in which we now, as a profession, can see that education is the greatest social tool available. To seek to close gaps of disadvantage, we place much more value on ensuring that all students are culturally and academically enriched in school and are able to leave school with the same knowledge as those in more privileged social contexts. Pastoral care underpins all of this: it can broaden horizons; it can develop students' effort and motivation; it can build resilience; it can develop confidence. Truly, it is the springboard from which students can have their lives changed through learning.

There are some key concepts on which pastoral leaders need to be fully informed. These range from the areas of cognitive science through to the evidence around effort and motivation, and pastoral leaders must ensure their own knowledge of these key concepts is strong so that they can implement provision that will directly impact on the academic success of their students.

Effort

If there is one thing that unites teenagers, it is the concept of effort. Too often teenagers are stereotyped as lazy, and their understanding of the concept of effort often benefits from some external development. That is not to say that teenagers lack the ability to put effort in; far from it. It is to say, however, that many young people lack a concrete understanding of what the word 'effort' has come to mean. Combine this with the near certainty that at some stage in their educational journey they will be told by a well-meaning person to 'put more effort in' and you have a recipe for them not really knowing how to improve very much at all.

I'd be willing to bet you too have told a student this at some stage; I know I have. Early on in my career, it was my go-to area for improvement for students, especially at GCSE, where exams were lurking around the corner.

'Put more effort in,' I'd say, beaming away, thinking I was being helpful.

It took me a few years to understand that this was, in fact, quite an unhelpful thing to say.

What does effort look like?

What exactly should I be doing?

How should I use my time?

Those are all things that are not detailed in the catch-all 'putting in more effort'. Imagine one of your students who you know needs to be putting more effort in. Can you clearly and concisely tell them how to do this?

Could they tell you what it is they should be doing?

It's not easy, not at all.

Defining effort is key, to ourselves as professionals but also to our students. This is where pastoral care should lean on the shoulders of giants and be informed by experts in cognitive science. Within this domain, effort is defined as 'using more mental energy for any given unit of time – not just using more time' by Professor John Dunlosky (2020, p. 2), a leading expert in this field.

Whilst definitions help us in our understanding of a concept, we also need to explore what this means in practice for students.

Dunlosky (2020) goes on to argue that effort in and of itself is not responsible for achievement, something that may well come as a surprise to us and to our young people. It seems to be an accepted adage in schools that the more effort you put in the better you do.

If this isn't the case, what *does* make the difference?

Dunlosky suggests it is what students are doing that has a causal impact on their learning, rather than the effort that is invested. Put simply, we need students to be working in the right ways rather than simply putting in 'more effort'. If they are spending hours of time working on things that do not help them learn, their effort will not translate into outcomes. It is concepts such as these that I believe all students deserve to be aware of; they need to know how best to spend their 'coin of the learning realm' (Dunlosky 2020, p. 2).

How does this translate to pastoral care?

Quite easily – it's something we need to be upfront about with students, especially in terms of the frequency with which we talk about learning with them. This is the kind of concept we should teach explicitly to students. Often, there may be a conscious – or subconscious – divide in schools between 'teaching and learning' and 'pastoral care', with the two camps neatly defined.

This is the wrong approach. One (teaching and learning) is underpinned by the other (pastoral care).

This has meant that traditional CPD for pastoral leaders may not focus on core academic knowledge we need to have. Indeed, this is knowledge I have amassed through many years of engagement with academic research, reading papers and journals, and through voluntary conferences where content such as this is shared. Where we have teaching pastoral leaders, the transfer of this knowledge should happen more seamlessly than it perhaps has in the past. We, as pastoral leaders, teaching or non-teaching, should be the manifestation of knowledge. We need to have amassed a whole range of knowledge about learning so that we can best know how to support our young people.

That alone, however, won't solve the issues.

This is where working collaboratively with academic middle leaders can have the most leverage. We can ensure that this concept is recapped in subject lessons; we can ensure that all students are taught, explicitly, and taught how to be doing the right things, rather than being simply told to put in more effort.

The concept of effort as I've outlined here is a perfect example of the way in which pastoral care should work in tandem with teaching and learning. The role of the pastoral leader should be as academic as that of any other leader. But what is it we need to know about? Let me give you a guided tour around the areas that stand to benefit us the most.

Retrieval practice

In 2006, a seminal and influential paper was published by Roediger and Karpicke. Entitled 'The Power of Testing Memory: Basic research and implications for educational practice', this paper has become somewhat of a classic in the teaching and learning world. It sought to compare different methods of study and testing on material that students were using, by looking at their performance based on the methods used.

What they found was significant for anyone involved in supporting learning. Their findings showed that students had better recall of the content they were studying if they were tested on the content they were studying after they had studied it.

They went on to discover that this testing advantage was only present after a two-day or one-week delay between studying and testing. Interestingly, they found that if testing took place immediately after study, the testing had no positive impact. In fact, students only studying, with no form of testing, went on to perform better. This has further been tested in a range of other studies.

Butler (2010) tested the concept further, finding that, in the study of the learning of texts, questions on a passage from a text also improved students' ability to transfer ideas to other contexts. This suggests that retrieval practice can help students' wider learning and development, supporting a broader understanding.

Retrieval practice as a concept, then, is something that students should be aware of. It is also something they should be engaged in regularly, given the potential impact on their learning and performance. Often, there is a narrative within education, and equally amongst students, that testing is inherently bad. This is not the case – quite the opposite, clearly. The negative narrative around testing stems from the social, often learnt behaviour, of stress.

Young people learn from the adults around them that testing is stressful, and they therefore learn to equate the two. This is an unhelpful narrative. Whilst it's clear that we all feel stress or pressure in significant moments such as GCSE examinations, it's important that students, teachers, and parents know that this regular, strategic, low-stakes retrieval practice happens regularly because it helps learning. It is not a stressful experience and it does not need to be viewed as one. In fact, we need to help students to see that there is nothing to fear and everything to be grateful for in terms of regular, low-stakes testing. Furthermore, these methods of testing often help build students' positive experiences of learning and help them to believe in their own knowledge and achievement. They can tangibly see when they make progress, and, crucially, what it is that they do not yet know well enough.

As professionals in school, how we talk about stress in relation to exams and testing also needs significant care and attention. This affects us, as pastoral leaders, but also all adults our students work with. Stress is contagious: the more we talk about stress negatively, the more space we allow it to fill, the more this feeling will become passed on to our students. We have to create an atmosphere where students can openly and honestly discuss stress and their mental health, but crucially not create an atmosphere where doing so only serves to exacerbate the very issue at hand. Needless to say, it is a difficult balance to strike. This is something to plan for, especially if you work with upper school students. We have a role to play in students' lives around educating them about stress, but also in helping them manage it, as well as acknowledging that it is a healthy bodily response that we can be proactive with ourselves.

How can I use this in pastoral care?

- Teach students about learning and the role retrieval practice plays in it.
- Give students time within your pastoral provision to engage in retrieval practice, especially at crucial exam and assessment points.
- Ensure form tutors have a confident understanding of the concept and can model it with students regularly.
- Plan for, and actively manage, the way in which you will deal with stress in students, especially in upper year groups.

Ebbinghaus's Forgetting Curve

Ebbinghaus's 1880 study into the concept of forgetting is a classic. Its impact on the field of psychology, and, in turn, learning, is undeniable. Influenced heavily by the work of the German philosopher Herbart, Ebbinghaus was the first to research the way in which forgetting works in the brain. Through his work, he sought to define the way in which we forget. As his work progressed, he began to explore the 'shape' of forgetting. A fascinating picture emerged, one which suggested, for the first time, not only the shape of forgetting, but the speed at which the human brain forgets.

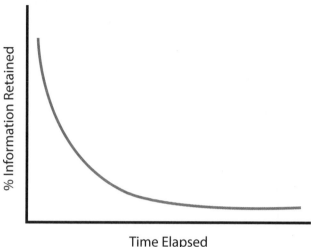

Time Elapsed

What Ebbinghaus's research showed, and what subsequent studies have replicated, won't come as a surprise, but it is a seminal text nonetheless, in part because of its status as the first exploration of forgetting showing that, over time, we retain less and less previously learnt information. It also shows us that the biggest drop in retention happens very quickly after learning – an important concept for students to be aware of. All too often, in my experience, students worry that they forget lesson content quickly. They mistakenly equate their own ability and progress with what is actually the human brain just doing what it has always done. Unchecked, it can become a monster that eats away at their self-confidence. It's important, therefore, that they are aware that this is a normal function of the human brain. The old saying goes that 'Knowledge is Power'; knowledge of the inner workings of the mind is too, if you ask me.

Ebbinghaus's early work is a great example of research that tells us there is a problem. What matters equally is what the field can also tell us about defying this natural disadvantage. With his initial curve showing that the biggest drop in retention of learning happens quickly after the initial learning, he also discovered the concept of 'spaced learning' – essentially, reviewing learning soon after the original period of learning, and doing this regularly. Ebbinghaus found that the initial session should happen when recall has fallen significantly, but crucially not at a point where retention has fallen so low that you are essentially starting from scratch. This concept is most easily understood, especially by students, as a graphic.

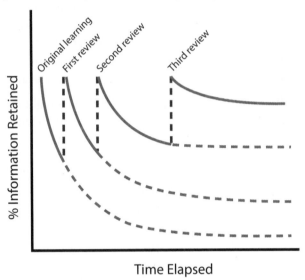

As you can see here, Ebbinghaus's work concluded that regular recap and restudy will help strengthen the learning that takes place.

As we know all too well, too many students either mistakenly believe that they can cram learning into a short space of time in the build-up to high-pressure assessments or that they will simply just miraculously remember everything from years of study. This is where we need to educate students more explicitly about how we learn, and about how they can work to ensure they have the best chances of being successful.

How can I use this in pastoral care?

- Teach students explicitly about this.
- Revisit the concept regularly – practise what you preach!
- Use the findings to help support students through high-stress periods – in this case, knowledge is power, and the more that

students can understand the workings of their own minds, the more they will succeed.

Optimal distributed practice

We've established some of the key concepts in learning that students should be supported with through pastoral provision. In the previous example, Ebbinghaus established the idea that recapping learning regularly helped to minimise the extent to which we might forget it. What it doesn't do, however, is tell us precisely what time frames we should be exploring, other than ensuring that key concepts are recapped at an early stage.

In their now influential paper, Cepeda et al. (2009) sought to explore the regularity with which recap of learning could help our retention of it – in short, the optimal intervals for retaining information.

Time before test	Optimum interval between study sessions
1 week	1–2 days
1 month	1 week
2 months	2 weeks
6 months	3 weeks
1 year	4 weeks

This paper details a more strategic approach we can use, not only as teachers in curriculum planning, but also with students, to help them understand the process of long-term learning. This can give clear direction as to how best students can create conditions for their own success.

How can I use this in pastoral care?

- Ensure students are taught explicitly about this.
- Talk regularly to students about their learning.
- Provide time where study resources such as flash cards and self-quizzing can be made and used.
- Ensure your tutors and pastoral team are well trained and understand the theory behind what you're implementing.
- Create revision planning, underpinned by the principles explored here, so that students have a clear, easy to follow, appropriately spaced revision schedule in the build-up to high-stakes assessments.

One of the things that often surprises me, when ensuring that support such as this is in place for students, is the idea that this isn't the purpose of pastoral care; we should stay in our lane.

Imagine for a moment that you are responsible for year 11, arguably the most important year of education that young people experience.

This is a period when students often experience high levels of stress and pressure, some of which are internal and some of which are external. They need extra care and compassion to support their mental health. They struggle with the anxiety that exams inevitably bring. They don't sleep properly. They stop eating healthily.

This is the exact opposite of what we want for any of our students; this absolutely *is* a pastoral concern.

We must look at how best we might create conditions where fewer students are impacted in this way.

Think about when you have experienced stressful situations when you've had high-stakes exams or assessments. How do you get in control?

By planning for it, creating a routine, creating structure, and following the plan for implementing it.

For our students to be able to do the same, and create the best conditions for their mental health to thrive, we have a duty of care to ensure that they have a full and clear knowledge of the science of learning. Alongside this, we have a duty of care to give our students access to expert support in working towards these significant life events. If one of our goals in education is to ensure that students leave school with the doors open for their next steps in life, we need to create the conditions for them to do so.

The very best pastoral care in a school underpins teaching and learning, leading to life-changing outcomes for our students. We do this best when we create pastoral systems that merge this seamlessly, where our provision strengthens the work that classroom teachers are doing day in, day out. By teaching students more explicitly about the science of how they learn, we are equipping them with the power to change their lives through learning.

Motivation

Creating motivated learners is the gold standard for anyone working in schools. We know the success that can follow when students are highly motivated. Understanding the concept of motivation, then, is key in our pursuit of this. To do so, we must look towards the research and evidence base to help us in our understanding of what motivation is and how we can best harness it in schools.

If we start with exploring the importance of motivation, we might look at Mccrea (2020, p. 8), who states that 'motivation influences behaviour, learning and wellbeing. It is an upstream cause of behaviour'. Much in the same way that I have outlined so far, this is another concept that could all too easily be seen as the domain of the classroom teacher and the academic middle leaders. In reality, motivation is a core concept that pastoral leaders need to be equally well versed on. We are uniquely placed to know the struggles our young people face; so, too, do we know their ambitions and aspirations. We owe it to them to ensure we are well informed in how best we support them through the challenges they face to give them the very best chance of achieving their dreams.

Motivation, much in the same way as effort and learning, is, frustratingly, an invisible entity. We cannot see it; we cannot mould it; we cannot easily define it. This adds a layer of complexity to what we are trying to achieve.

However, the importance of getting it right in schools cannot be underestimated. In 2008, The Education Endowment Foundation (EEF) published a review of metacognition and self-regulation, which detailed the importance of motivation in learning.

In the EEF documents, there is a synthesis of research and evidence bases, accompanied by recommendations they make on the back of this for school leaders and teachers.

In one of their metacognition report recommendations, they state that schools should ensure that they 'explicitly teach pupils how to organise and effectively manage their learning independently: Teachers should also support pupils' motivation to undertake the learning tasks'.

Whilst the onus is on classroom teachers to work with students within the subject domain, pastoral systems also provide a vital opportunity to develop students' motivation further.

As with other largely invisible concepts in learning, it helps to initially define what we seek to understand. Mccrea (2020, p. 18) describes motivation as 'a system for allocating attention'. However, he also argues that the mechanics of motivation are highly complex, and it is this complexity that is at the root of a widescale lack of clarity around motivation, both in general and in schools. He goes on to argue that the answer lies in the science of motivation. In the text, he explores this and surmises that there are 'core drivers' of motivation that we can implement in schools.

They are:

Secure success. He argues that giving students a high success rate in school to look back on is key, as it is framing what success means and helping students to attribute it accurately, as well as pre-empting failure.

Run routines. He argues that we must make the process of learning easy, whilst keeping the content of learning challenging.

Nudge norms. This would include elevating the visibility of desirable norms, amplifying peer approval, and putting emphasis on what we want to happen, rather than outlining what we do not want to happen.

Build belonging. This includes developing a unifying purpose and creating a common ground within a group, as well as earning and keeping trust.

Boost buy-in. This suggests that exposing the benefits of the choices you make for students, as well as providing opportunities for them to buy into what you're doing, can help bolster motivation.

As you can see, some of these lend themselves well to classroom-based practice. However, there are clear areas where pastoral care can contribute to building motivation in our students. So how might we do that, and what might we focus on?

Secure success

Here, as a leader of a year group, building a narrative of success is key. There are multiple opportunities to do this, through assemblies, through form time discussion topics, through to external speakers. The more you can build a culture of success, the more students will feel they are able to be successful themselves. We should also be acutely aware of students' prior attainment. As Coe et al. (2014, p. 23) suggest, 'the poor motivation of low attainers is a logical response to repeated failure'. This makes sense. If our students go through their time at secondary school, and indeed even earlier, experiencing an inability to access the curriculum fully, or struggling with basic reading and writing, of course their motivation will be impacted. We must know our students indelibly well and know precisely where our efforts in building success must be placed.

Run routines

As a pastoral leader, you may find that there are whole school routines you play a key role in. These are best revisited regularly. However, in some schools, there may be significantly fewer whole school routines and more flexibility for you as a pastoral leader to create your own within certain parts of the school day. Consider what habits you want to build in your students, what key routines you need them in at certain parts of the day, or even the routines that class teachers might need them in that you can support through your pastoral provision. The more regularly we can establish, reinforce, and remind students of routines, the more motivated and successful that can be.

Nudge norms

This is a key aspect for pastoral leaders. There are an infinite number of ways you can do this. From the way you create and craft your expectation, vision, and culture as a pastoral leader (see Chapter 2), through to the individual conversations that you have with students, or through visiting students in lessons, almost all communication with students is an opportunity to develop this further.

Build belonging

This is probably one of the clearest areas for a pastoral leader. This is what we do – we create a culture for a year group, and we spearhead it. We are leading students, with their individual lives, contexts, and studies, through to success. We create an identity for this, and we generate conditions whereby every student can feel they belong. This is a key concept, especially with our most disengaged or apathetic learners. Deci and Ryan's (1985) Self-Determination Theory is also significant here, focusing on 'relatedness' – the desire to have positive relationships. This is a well-supported theory, with Pink's (2011) motivation-focussed text *Drive: The surprising truth about what motivates us* also focussing closely on the importance of creating the drive and desire to feel part of something bigger. If we can create a culture in our year groups where this drive and desire exist, we will reap the rewards of a more motivated group of young people striving to achieve their aims.

Boost buy-in

This is also at the heart of a lot of what we do as pastoral leaders. We have countless opportunities to do this. In my experience, I have found that talking openly and directly to students about what I am doing as their pastoral leader, and why I am taking those decisions, helps them to understand the bigger picture. We see this time and time again in human behaviour. When we understand the rationale, we are more open to playing our role within it.

Although this has been a somewhat brief tour of what I would coin seminal research, there is a huge wealth of inspiration around for us to draw on as pastoral leaders. We owe it to our young people to make the best bets we can with the time we have with them. This time is limited and short in the grand scheme of things. Our young people only get one shot at this. We have a moral imperative, therefore, to use what evidence can tell us to create the optimal conditions for success in our young people. In doing so, we seek to ensure that students are successful, happy learners who can experience success in school. This, without question, is a core part of our role as pastoral leaders.

Practical strategies

Whilst having a strong knowledge of research and evidence is important, so too is the ability to implement it within your context so that the benefits of it can be experienced by our students.

Parental engagement

One of the most powerful moments in my career development was a line management meeting. I realise how strange that sounds – but it was such a formative moment for me as a pastoral leader. My then line manager (deputy head Dr Michelle Henley) and I were discussing our shared frustration with my year group, whose levels of apathy towards a mock exam period were astronomical.

Between us, rather than letting this frustration fester and develop, we quickly decided that we had to do something. This moment, for me, cemented the idea that a core part of leadership in general, but one that is vital to pastoral leadership, is the ability to do something about, or in reaction to, something. We are in control of how we respond to challenges.

In this case, we decided upon a parental engagement strategy, and tying this more widely to a series of lessons and assemblies focussing on learning and success. Within four weeks, we held a highly attended parents' information evening, during which we essentially taught parents the same evidence informed learning strategies we were teaching to students.

Alongside this, we covered more generic ways that parents could support learning at home, whilst also increasing the profile of the impact of regular study on long-term learning. Parents largely bought in, and so did students. Quite quickly, we had a much more powerful approach in place, and it is something we have refined and evolved as we have developed as a school. Engaging parents in this way, for me, is a vital cog in the wheel of supporting our students.

Working collaboratively

As we have seen, most of the evidence and research falls naturally more within the teaching and learning realm. However, not much succeeds in isolation; the same is true of improving provision in school for students. A lot of this, though, will depend on our own context and school. In an ideal world, you'd be in a school with a strong teaching and learning team, also rowing in the same direction with evidence informed provision. If that's you, work with them. Bolster your provision together. Pioneer a pastoral and academic hybrid of support – I promise you won't regret it. If you are not in that position, going it alone is better than not going at all. We don't all work in the perfect world, but I would hope that as a pastoral leader you have the autonomy to drive forward for your provision in new and innovative ways. Build it, and they will come.

Pastoral curriculum

This is a concept I have touched on several times. Your pastoral curriculum, whether you have a formalised document or not, whether you are even aware of your curriculum or not, does exist. We all have one. This is something I would argue every pastoral leader should be thinking about and developing rather than simply leaving it to chance.

This doesn't have to be a significant piece of work. It doesn't need to be a bastardised tube map of interconnected knowledge. It should, however, be informed by the needs and experiences of your young people, as well as by their context and your own community.

A good place to start would be to spend some time mapping out key dates and moments in your year group's journey with you. Use this to dictate what needs to be covered and when. For example, covering the science of learning four weeks before GCSE examinations start isn't going to cut it – that's something you need to front load in Key Stage 4 and continue to build and recap over time, so that when those high-profile moments come around, and they do so rapidly, your students are well-versed experts in what you need them to know.

There will be other aspects to this too; your pastoral curriculum is about developing a rounded experience for young people. Do they need some careers provision? What about stress management? Is their cultural capital where it should be? Are they getting enough opportunities to read and be read to?

They're all questions to consider for yourself and ultimately for your students, in your contexts. Be informed by them and their needs.

Case study

Imagine you are a head of year, about to take on a year 10 year group, taking them through to year 11. You are aware they are apathetic. They have a bit of a reputation within the school as lacking direction and focus. You're now planning for your time with them, orchestrating and building a culture of success.

Note down:

What would be your aims?

What key points in the two-year journey are priorities?

What would you cover with them in your pastoral provision, and when?

What principles of cognitive science would you want to teach them about?

How will you generate effort in your students?

How will you build motivation?

What other milestones do students experience on this journey with you?

What do you need them to buy into?

How will you create and build something that all students want to be part of?

Key Learning Points

1. Pastoral care and academic progress are too often seen as opposites.
2. Pastoral care and academic progress should work symbiotically within a school, with the pastoral care provision playing a leading role in supporting students.
3. We need to teach students explicitly about learning behaviours, and how best to create conditions for academic success.
4. Students should be taught about the brain and how we learn, as well as knowing how to work with our natural weaknesses and how to overcome them.
5. There are key areas of research that students should know about: retrieval practice, forgetting, spacing, effort, and motivation.
6. Pastoral leaders are uniquely placed to develop motivation across an entire cohort.
7. Pastoral leaders are the architects of culture and behaviour.

RECOMMENDED READING

Alongside the texts already mentioned, there are several texts that have had a formative impact on my development of pastoral provision. These texts focus more specifically on the theme of learning.

Kirschner, P.A. and Hendrick, C. (2020). *How Learning Happens: Seminal works in educational psychology and what they mean in practice*. London and New York, NY: Routledge.

This text is truly excellent. It provides an in-depth exploration of a range of psychology and cognitive science core works that all of us working with young people's learning should be aware of. It is a must read.

Didau, D. and Rose, D. (2016). *What Every Teacher Needs to Know About Psychology*. Woodbridge: John Catt Educational.

This is another excellent text designed at upskilling professionals and widening our knowledge of research and evidence that we can make best use of in schools. The book itself takes quite complex domains of research and makes these accessible and easy for busy professionals.

Willingham, D. (2021). *Why Don't Students Like School? A cognitive scientist answers questions about how the mind works*. Second edition. Hoboken, NJ: Jossey-Bass.

This text was initially somewhat ahead of its time, especially in the English education system. Now a vital part of our professional repertoire, this text is full of helpful and insightful information. This book was my gateway into a new world of understanding when it comes to learning.

Sumeracki, M. and Weinstein, Y. (2019). *Understanding How We Learn: A visual guide*. Abingdon: Routledge.

This text, written by the Learning Scientists, was born after their hugely successful website www.learningscientists.org became a leading source of information on evidence informed practice for teachers.

Hendrick, C. (2018), on his blog www.chronotopeblog.com, makes use of the aforementioned Learning Scientists, and summarises a range of research in an excellent, accessible blog post, alongside a widely used study guide for students based on the principles of cognitive science. We made use of this in our school, providing copies to both parents and students. Its greatest strength lies in its simplicity – it can be easily understood and accessed by parents and students alike.

REFERENCES

Butler, J. (2010). Repeated Testing Produces Superior Transfer of Learning Relative to Repeated Studying, *Journal of Experimental Psychology: Learning, Memory, and Cognition*, 36(5), pp. 1118–1133.

Cepeda, N.J., Vul, E., Rohrer, D., Wixted, J.T. and Pashler, H. (2009). Spacing effects in learning: A temporal ridgeline of optimal retention, *Psychological Science*, 11, pp. 1095–1102.

Coe, R., Aloisi, C., Higgins, S. and Major, L.E. (2014). What Makes Great Teaching? A review of the underpinning research. Project Report. London: Sutton Trust.

Deci, E.L. and Ryan, R.M. (1985). *Intrinsic Motivation and Self-determination in Human Behaviour*. New York, NY: Plenum Press.

Didau, D. and Rose, D. (2016). *What Every Teacher Needs to Know About Psychology*. Woodbridge: John Catt Educational.

Education Endowment Foundation (2020). *Metacognition and Self-Regulated Learning*. Available at: https://educationendowmentfoundation. org.uk/public/files/Publications/Metacognition/EEF_Metacognition_ and_self-regulated_learning.pdf. Accessed 24 July 2021.

Dunlosky, J., Badali, S., Rivers, M.L. and Rawson, K. (2020). The Role of Effort in Understanding Educational Achievement: Objective effort as an explanatory construct versus effort as a student perception, *Educational Psychology Review*, 32, pp. 1163–1175.

Ebbinghaus, H. (1908). *Psychology: An elementary textbook*. New York, NY: Arno Press.

Hendrick, C. (2018). www.chronotopeblog.com.

Kirschner, P.A. and Hendrick, C. (2020). *How Learning Happens: Seminal works in educational psychology and what they mean in practice*. London and New York, NY: Routledge.

Mccrea, P. (2020). *Motivated Teaching: Harnessing the science of motivation to boost attention and effort in the classroom*. pepsmccrea. com.

Murre, J.M.J. and Dros, J. (2015). Replication and Analysis of Ebbinghaus' Forgetting Curve, *PLoS ONE* 10(7): e0120644. Available at: https://doi. org/10.1371/journal.pone.0120644. Accessed 24 July 2021.

Pink, D. (2011). *Drive: The Surprising Truth About What Motivates Us*. Edinburgh: Canongate Books Ltd.

Roediger, H. and Karpicke, J.D. (2006). The Power of Testing Memory: Basic research and implications for educational practice, *Perspectives on Psychological Science*, 1(3), pp. 181–210.

Sumeracki, M. and Weinstein, Y. (2019). *Understanding How We Learn: A visual guide*. Abingdon: Routledge.

Willingham, D. (2021). *Why Don't Students Like School? A cognitive scientist answers questions about how the mind works*. Second edition. Hoboken, NJ: Jossey-Bass.

CHAPTER 5
ATTENDANCE

A child's attendance at school is one of the most important factors in their education. The correlation between attendance and outcomes has a long, borne out history. Those that attend well tend to achieve well, broadly speaking. They are immersed in the curriculum daily, making academic progress each day. Not only does this lead to increased learning, but it also leads, in my experience, to improved academic self-esteem. Students who attend school consistently see the benefits; they learn; they make progress; and, as a result, they have an increasing positivity towards their achievements. They're able to build upon previous learning and continue to learn. As well as this, the social impacts are clear. They often maintain peer relationships well; they're a constant in one another's lives. The more they miss, the more their peer relationships can suffer. I've often observed this from a distance as a pastoral leader. Students miss out on collective moments, they miss out on significant peer group moments, and they miss out on the socialising that takes place at breaks and lunch times. When students become a less predictable presence, their friendships can sometimes suffer.

Despite it being one of the single most important contributors to success, it is also one of the most frustrating aspects of pastoral care in my experience. There are many background factors that contribute to poor attendance. Furthermore, it is something that is deeply personal to students and their families – whilst the reasons for lower attendance may be similar, the way they manifest themselves in students and their families is often different. Exploring this with students and their families takes time, patience, compassion, and tenacity. The most important thing that a pastoral leader can do is to establish the kind of relationship with a student, and with their family, whereby the reasons for low attendance are clear and can be discussed without fear or judgement. The most frequent factors can be:

Academic

Students' learning is a deeply personal experience, one that is indelibly tied to their own mental health, wellbeing, and emotional welfare. Where students have academic difficulties, learning becomes an ever-growing challenge in their lives.

Sometimes this can be from a known learning difficulty, or SEND (Special Educational Needs and Disabilities). Oftentimes, however, academic progress and attendance turn into a vicious cycle. Students' low attendance means they miss learning. When they return to school, they are academically behind. Reintegrating becomes a problem. They go from lesson to lesson seeing their better-attending peers have less difficulty with their learning. They go from lesson to lesson feeling behind. They experience less and less success, whereas those around them seem to experience more. This becomes their 'normal' – it's how they perceive the average school experience when, in fact, it is often the opposite. This can, in turn, lead to further attendance issues. No one enjoys feeling behind, or not accessing the curriculum. Motivation to attend school can drop – and the cycle becomes ever more vicious, with further gaps appearing and attendance often continuing to fall.

Parental

Many of us have, as adults, formed a world view of school and of education. Most have been to school at some point in our lives – and this is in the formative stages in our lives, where our experiences shape us as we grow into adults.

Every parent, step-parent, grandparent, and carer will have developed their own world views too. For some, their relationship with schools and with authority is damaged before their child even gets to us. Perhaps they had a particularly difficult time at school themselves. Perhaps they were bullied. Perhaps they had negative relationships with authority figures. Perhaps they began to detach from the importance of learning.

It is this we must remember when we are dealing with students and their families. Without seeking to understand the mental dynamics towards school and education that our students are influenced by and immersed in, we will rarely find positive, impactful ways to help them attend school more regularly. This is, I would argue, one of the single most important factors in working with students to improve their attendance. It is also a time-consuming, relational act – it takes time, effort, and tenacity to build relationships with families whereby attitudes to learning can be explored, openly and honestly, and positive ways forward established from this.

Health

Students' physical and mental health impacts on their attendance in a number of ways. From hospital appointments to other genuine health needs, attendance will be impacted in ways that are seldom within the control of our students. Students in this category can also be acutely aware of their conditions and how they negatively impact on their lives. We know that the best message for students is that they need to be in school. It is the best place for them. However, we must consider that within our cohorts we have students facing a whole raft of different barriers to attendance, and those with long-term or serious health conditions need careful thought, both in terms of what is right for them and in the way we talk publicly about attendance. This is especially true where blanket policies such as rewards for 100% attendance come into force.

Imagine, for example, you have a physical disability for which you need to see your consultant three times a year – these times are dictated to you by your condition and by your consultant. Your consultant is based in a hospital that is 90 minutes away – your appointment, which is vital to your health, means that you'll miss most of a day at school.

It'll be authorised, of course. But it will mean that, even if you manage, despite all the challenges you face, to attend school well despite these appointments, you'll never get to 100% because of factors way beyond your control. You'll never get an award, even if you manage to attend every day except for when you're seeing your consultant.

It's not hard to see how this becomes a significant drain on your perseverance and commitment to attend school. This is where schools, and pastoral leaders, must seek to make appropriate reasonable adjustments and deal with attendance at an individual level. It can be a small number of students that this impacts in your cohort, but it is nonetheless a significant part of supporting those students to feel positive about their attendance at school.

I remember from my own time at school just how important this responsive approach can be. When I was in year 9, my dad spent a good few months in Intensive Care in a hospital in the next county. It was the nearest specialist bed for him. I remember my head teacher at the time, a very wonderful man, pulling me to one side one day. I thought I was in trouble, but the reality was quite the opposite. All he said to me was that he knew school wasn't my priority right now, and to take whatever time I needed. I attended school every single day after that, not because anyone had told me to, but because there was a bit of compassion and understanding there. This is the impact we have as professionals in schools; knowing your students and knowing what to say and who to say it to are vital. I can think of countless students in my time where that conversation would have led to some pretty catastrophic attendance. But he pitched it perfectly.

Ultimately, when it comes to attendance, we are dealing with human beings, each with their own experiences and challenges. Human beings are rarely straightforward!

Bullying and peer relationships

We know, as adults, that we are more likely to want to be somewhere where we feel valued, important, and cared for by the people we are around. The same is true for students, perhaps even more so for children than it is for adults, such is the intense importance of peer group relationships at that age.

Where relationships and friendships might have broken down, or where bullying is taking place, this can also exacerbate attendance issues. As a pastoral leader, you need to have your finger on the pulse here – you need to know your cohort inside out and be in tune with friendship groups. This can often be an early indicator of things going wrong – it's the kind of soft data you gather informally through your day-to-day interactions with students and by simply being a presence in and around social times.

Where bullying is a concern, it is vital that you have established a culture where students can let a trusted adult know they have a concern. This may not always be you – it may be a form tutor, a teacher, a pastoral support worker. Anyone the child trusts. Every child should have a champion within a school, someone who is there for them to open up to when they are experiencing difficulties.

This isn't solely about bullying – it can be about anything. Bullying does, however, tend to be an area that students can feel vulnerable talking about. This can apply in the home too. It takes a lot of courage for students to open up about it – therefore, your response as a pastoral leader, and as a school, holds a lot of weight. There needs to be a culture where action is taken promptly, and where students know that their concerns will be listened to and taken seriously. You have a key role in this as a pastoral leader, and it is important that your actions speak with the same volume as your words. You also need to demonstrate that you are listening as well as acting. There will be times when students want you to do nothing; you must respect that, even if you disagree. The dynamics of this initial opening up need to be maintained – the student needs to feel safe and in control. The very nature of bullying means that they lack control over their lives as it is, without us then making it worse. Keep that in mind when students open up.

Socio-economic

Students' home lives can impact on attendance for all manner of reasons. We must never make assumptions here; the root cause may not be linked to attitudes to education, but more to the circumstances of their lives. Oftentimes we know precious little about a child's life, often knowing only what they want us to know. Where there are influences in the home on students' attendance, time must be taken to understand more about these.

It's important not to make assumptions when it comes to socio-economic influences on attendance. Too often, we use too narrow a lens, for example, by focussing on Pupil Premium students and making blanket assumptions about students.

It may be that there are childcare issues in the home, with older siblings playing a role in the childcare arrangements of their younger siblings. It may be that there is an event in school that is a financial impossibility for the family – a school trip, a food tech lesson, a cake sale, a non-uniform day. All of these can contribute to attendance difficulties in different ways. Therefore, knowing your students and their parents, and being non-judgemental and approachable as a pastoral leader, are important tools in your kit. It can be difficult for anyone to open up and talk about financial issues – and, from your perspective, it needs to be handled in a tactful way.

What these barriers have in common is the importance of knowing your students, and the culture that you create as a pastoral leader, both within school for the student and out of school towards parents. In Chapter 2, I explored the deliberate construction of culture and vision. In many respects, this is similar, except the culture you're creating is the one parents and carers are on the receiving end of, rather than students themselves. Consider the messages they get from you – both the public and the private.

Are they warm and supportive? Do they allow for ease of communication with you? How are you crafting a culture in which parents can and do feel they can talk openly about any difficulties they face? Is it easy to contact you? Do all parents have a way to contact you that works for them? Do they know that you can help?

Defining attendance problems

Attendance is one area where there are clear parameters around defining the problem. Equally, it is also something your school will be judged on – and rightly so. One of the key parts of attendance in any school comes from gathering the right data, on the right things, which is reported at the right time. Generally speaking, this should be weekly, with a monthly and half termly profile too. It must inform you of individual students' attendance so that you are able to work with those who require input. In essence, categories of attendance can be broken down as:

Above 96%: Attendance is considered good. However, keep a close eye on those towards the lower end.

90–96%: This is a concern. Contact should be made with the family to ensure they are aware of concerns. This can be via phone, via letter, via text message – the means is best decided by knowing your context and your families. This needs careful and regular monitoring, especially where attendance may continue to decrease. Where it increases, it's important to notice that too and to praise it.

85–89%: Significant concern. At this stage, a few things need to be in place:

- Contact made with the family around the seriousness of the issue.
- A meeting in school with the student and their family to discuss barriers to attendance and strategies for improvement.
- An agreement that all medical absences will be evidenced, either by an appointment card or a prescription/medication proof. Contact must be made on every day of absence to hold the family to account to this agreement.
- Proceed in line with your local arrangements regarding fixed penalty notices. These vary between counties and local authorities. Work with your school experts as well as those involved from other agencies where appropriate.

Below 80%: At this stage, attendance this low is a real concern. Sometimes, attendance at this rate may be unavoidable – a student may have had surgery or another genuine health issue. However, where genuine issues are not known, an attendance panel should be held, with relevant stakeholders in attendance. This should include a member of your senior leadership team and any local authority staff such as an Educational Welfare Officer. Again, local arrangements vary massively across the country, so this may look different in your context. In some schools, where expertise allows, this might include a governor of the school, especially where they have a specific area of strength, such as being a well-known local employer who is able to talk openly and honestly about attendance issues in the workplace. It may be the case, for reasons of confidentiality, that they only attend part of the meeting. Clear, measurable targets need to be agreed at this meeting, and to be followed up. It is often best to consider attendance as a weekly percentage by this stage – the overall attendance figure can feel like a significant barrier. A half termly target may also provide more motivation than the overall attendance figure.

Your role as a pastoral leader

Attendance is a whole school issue, and, as such, should be led by a member of your senior team. You are a vital cog in the wheel here, alongside any attendance and welfare staff you may have in school. Arrangements for this differ hugely across schools, with models fitting individual and local need.

Generally speaking, there are a number of things that, as a pastoral leader, you should have in place and be doing in order to make a contribution to the effective improvement of attendance:

Data monitoring

There should be a mechanism in place in school whereby data is provided to enable you to act. This should be weekly. Build this into your time each week to ensure that you can digest the information, but also act quickly upon it where there are key things emerging from it. You will need to protect some time to do some proactive work with students. The data needs to inform your steps and to outline which students need to be a priority for you. If this isn't in place in your school, work with your school to create a mechanism for this. Data is readily available on Information Management Systems and can be collated quickly by admin staff.

First day contact

At the start of each half term, those students with emerging or persistent attendance issues should be clear. In a new academic year, make use of the previous academic year's data so that you can act promptly. Work within the systems in place in your school to identify which students need to have first day contact, even where the parent has contacted school regarding an absence. The aim of this is early intervention and to ensure that communication is in place promptly. Review this weekly and add and remove students as improvements or declines are seen in your data. It's important to have a clear strategy for these students and to use the information available to manage this in more personalised ways. For example, some parents may be difficult to contact via phone, or find it difficult to talk on the phone. Use text messages to allow for a method of communication that suits them – you may well find that you get better communication when you approach students and families in ways that work for them.

Know – and notice – your students

This is something I learnt early in my career from one of the best pastoral leaders I have ever worked with – Ian Routledge. As an acting head of year, I worked with Ian and learnt very early on the power that noticing things holds. It sounds obvious now. But the power of noticing is particularly prevalent in attendance; it formed a key part of an excellent strategy that Ian went on to develop in our school and it remains one of the more impactful initiatives that I've seen work to improve attendance. What I learnt from this was that, when it comes to attendance, it can be increasingly easy for students' relationship with the school, or indeed their perceived relationship with the school, to begin to fall apart.

If no one notices they aren't there, does it even matter, in their mind, whether they're attending or not?

It's not hard to see how this develops and gradually decimates a student's attendance.

Simply spotting a student in school and saying 'I'm really pleased to see you in today. I noticed you weren't in yesterday – is everything OK?' holds a lot of weight. It shows the student that someone cares about them at a time when they could easily create a narrative that no one does. Try to make sure you have a clear understanding of who will notice those with increasingly low attendance. You can't do it all, much as you might like. Seek out key adults in students' lives, find out who they like and who they value, and get them on side to play this crucial role. This was at the heart of Ian's strategy – simple but effective. Talk to kids. Notice them.

Involve parents

We've touched earlier on the significant role that parents hold when it comes to attendance. Their importance cannot be understated. An important thing to remember is that parents and students often reveal different information. When you speak to students about their attendance, or reason for absence, it's important to interrogate these, and to fact check them with parents. A quick call to verify a child's explanation can be an illuminating exercise in exploring barriers to learning. I would always approach this conversation from a supportive place. 'Hi, it's Josh's head of year. I noticed he was off yesterday, and I just wanted to check if everything is OK?' is a much more gentle approach than saying 'Josh told me he had sinusitis – is this true?' One is likely to get you further than the other. Planning your communications, whilst knowing enough about students and their families to know how to pitch them, really helps prevent avoidable issues where communications end up doing more harm than good. Schools and families are only ever going to make progress with attendance where there is a positive working relationship. Don't ruin it with a badly pitched call – trust me on this one!

Target support

One key aspect of your role in the attendance jigsaw relies upon ensuring that the right support is in the right places, with the right people working with the right students. That might be a form tutor where there is a particularly strong relationship, or it might be an external agency in place through an Early Help. In essence, your role here is a bit like a conductor – you're directing the right support in the right places. It's important to remember that, as a pastoral leader, especially if you teach too, your time is limited, and you do need to draw on a range of avenues to get the right support in place. You can't solve all the issues, much as you might like to. You also don't have all the answers – a collaborative approach, drawing on the strengths of others, is vital. Your role lies in ensuring that everyone knows what their role is, and that you review and evaluate the impact of this regularly. Alongside this, the tenacity and perseverance of wanting to improve attendance through this targeted support is what makes the difference. Be the person that doesn't give – no child is beyond reach. We keep trying. Every. Single. Time. Learning is too important to waste it.

Positive reintegration

Getting students back into school can be a big enough job in and of itself. However, ensuring that this reintegration into school goes smoothly is paramount. There are always two sides to reintegration: the pastoral and the academic.

The pastoral is best explored with the student – do they need a daily check-in? Do they need some time out in inclusion? How will they manage social times? Focus here on the softer elements of their days.

In terms of the academic, your focus switches to their learning. Academic progress can be a big piece of the puzzle – you will need to ensure that there is support in place so that students can catch up and get support to fill in any gaps that might have emerged. Be sure to discuss this with their class teachers – they will know best the extent of the learning gap. Use their professional insights and expertise to help you formulate a plan that addresses this, along with their emotional and social support. It is also important to discuss this openly with students and ensure that they are well prepared in dealing with academic challenges. One thing worth remembering is that 'catch-up' is rarely as straightforward as we might like it to be. Especially for non-teaching staff, it could be easy to think that a few worksheets could solve the problem, but the classroom rarely works like that. Teaching is a live delivery – teachers deliver instruction, knowledge, and content. If students miss this, they miss out. It's incredibly hard to fix that gap and it is a significant ask on classroom teachers to expect them to fill these gaps. Work with them, not against them, and explore what they can realistically provide that can help the student reacclimatise into their lessons.

When discussing this with students before they go back into their lessons, there is a role for groundwork to prepare them to face any barriers that might emerge. How will they manage in their first lesson back if they don't understand what's happening? How will they ask for help in a busy classroom? What will they do if they get stuck?

These can all sound like easy things that they should be used to, but drawing attention to themselves, in what students often feel is a negative way, can also become a barrier itself. Work with them to work out what they'll do. Make sure their teachers are also fully informed of this, so that they can support your plans. It only takes a tiny knock to the confidence of students and the ramifications can be huge where attendance is a persistent issue, so keeping this in mind and being as proactive as possible in your planning is time well invested in the student's education.

Rewards and incentives

Rewards and incentives are somewhat commonplace in schools when it comes to attendance. From tickets to prom for year 11 students, to raffles and free bacon butties, there are all kinds of ways that schools try to incentivise good attendance. Whilst these can, sometimes, have an impact on some students, it is always important to explore this as a concept and consider the messages it sends, along with which students it rewards, and why.

One key aspect to a rewards-based approach to attendance that needs to be considered carefully in schools is around what we are rewarding students for. A very basic expectation in school is that all students attend school regularly. It's the law, for one. When we seek to reward this, are we, in fact, simply rewarding the basic standard? And, if so, do we undermine our own expectations of students in doing so?

Another consideration is who we reward, and why. Where students have made significant improvements in attendance, it can be easy to feel that a reward is warranted. Consider, however, for a moment, the impact that this might have on those students who attend school consistently. Are the expectations for them different?

It can easily become a minefield in terms of rewards.

A further consideration, as it should be with any strategy in school, is whether it actively seeks to improve what you are seeking to improve.

In their 2018 study, Robinson et al. of the Harvard Kennedy School of Government sought to evaluate the effectiveness of offering awards to motivate individual behaviour when it comes to attendance. Although carried out in the US, the study itself included over 15,000 students.

Surprisingly, given the backdrop around rewarding attendance in schools, they found that the prospective awards in schools did not, on average, improve attendance. More surprisingly, they found that retrospective awards for attendance actually decreased subsequent attendance.

In their exploration of their findings, the researchers suggest that awards may cause these unintended effects by inadvertently signalling that the target behaviour, perfect attendance, is neither the social norm nor the basic expectation of the school.

Furthermore, they suggest that with a retrospective award for attendance there is a suggestion to the recipients that they have already outperformed the norm, and therefore expectations of them – hence they miss school at a later date.

It is certainly an important and comprehensive study. As with any research, we should seek to be informed by it as something that can help us make the best bets for students in terms of the decisions we make in schools. It may go against our hunches in terms of what we feel we know about attendance and rewarding it. However, it is something we should, as pastoral leaders, critically engage with.

A further consideration that must be made, especially where attendance rewards are felt to be of benefit in a school, lies in who we reward. I explored earlier the context of a child with a long-term health issue or a lifelong disability. Where their attendance is beyond their control, is it right that we exclude them from rewards? I'd argue not.

Whatever you do in school, it is important to also have a filter to enable you to consider your personal knowledge of students, with any negative impact on them also forming part of the discussion around your provision.

Nudge Theory

One recently emerging theory around how we encourage certain behaviours from human beings is that of Nudge Theory. Originating from Richard Thaler and Cass Sunstein's 2008 book, *Nudge: Improving decisions about health, wealth, and happiness*, it centres on the apparent innovative, less coercive government interventions that have the potential to shape human behaviour. The book has gone on to be a surprise bestseller and its roots are being felt in an increasing number of approaches we see in society.

So, what exactly is a 'nudge'?

Thaler and Sunstein (2008) argue that people behave in ways that economic theory finds difficult to predict. This may well be unsurprising to those in our profession; too often we see the real-world ramifications of teenagers' ability to behave in unpredictable ways, oftentimes not in their best interest either.

This concept is also well supported in modern research (Kahneman 2011, Cialdini 2009, Ariely 2008). Whilst Thaler and Sunstein's (2008) work centres on the economic premise, the concept they first established has gone on to be used far more widely. Their definition is a helpful summary of the concept:

> A nudge, as we will use the term, is any aspect of the choice architecture that alters people's behaviour in a predictable way without forbidding any options or significantly changing their economic incentives. (p. 6)

They go on to say that: 'to count as a mere nudge, the intervention must be cheap and easy to avoid. Nudges are not mandates. Putting fruit at eye level (hoping that people then choose fruit over unhealthy alternatives) counts as a nudge. Banning junk food does not' (Thaler and Sunstein 2008, p. 6).

To put it more simply, it is a low-stakes intervention designed to prompt us to make so-called better decisions.

With a growing popularity in schools, given its low-cost premise, Nudge Theory has begun to emerge as an intervention to improve the choices made by students and parents.

Research such as that of Bettinger and Slonim (2007) demonstrates that children and adolescents are particularly likely to be 'influenced by self-control problems because their brains and particular executive functions are less developed' (Damgaard and Nielsen 2018, p. 315). Other research has linked this self-control issue to rates of dropout in education, primarily in the US, with Damgaard and Nielsen writing that 'empirical evidence suggests that individuals who are impatient are more likely to drop out of school' (p. 316).

Although the term 'dropout' is more Americanised, the issues between school attendance and dropping out are similar – one often leads to the other. These self-control issues can lead to poor decision-making. Furthermore, Damgaard and Nielson say the 'evidence suggests that, as with self-control problems, the effects of limited attention and cognitive ability are greater for low socio-economic status (SES) and attention problems and hyperactivity are related to reading difficulties and low academic achievement'.

With the picture increasingly suggesting that decision-making is an area where things can, evidently, go wrong, the decision of whether to attend school or not is one that can be affected in this way. Thus, the argument for use of Nudge Theory as an attendance strategy has begun to grow in schools.

An area of promise in research is around goal setting. In dealing with attendance, then, a key area where we might make use of Nudge Theory can be the setting of goals with both parents and students. In summarising the evidence base for this, Damgaard and Neilsen (2018, p. 321) suggest that 'goals become salient reference points that students (and parents) will be motivated to research to avoid psychological costs (due to loss aversion) of not reaching the goal. Therefore, asking students, parents and teachers to set a specific goal … may help alleviate self-control problems by subconsciously nudging individuals towards behaviour that enables them to meet the goal.'

Damgaard and Neilsen (2018, p. 325) also summarise the evidence around reminders as nudges. They conclude that 'studies nudging parents with reminders have almost consistently found positive effects on parental involvement and student skill.' There is scope, therefore, to engage parents in this way when dealing with attendance. Regular text messages reminding parents of the positive effects of good attendance is one method that schools could explore. It is relatively low cost, and the evidence base suggests that it could lead to a positive impact on how regularly children attend school.

Writing in their blog *An Evidence Informed Approach to Improving Attendance*, Durrington Research School have shared another strategy they have used that is also informed by Nudge Theory. Drawing on research in dentistry, they explore the idea that positive reinforcement of desirable behaviours can have a greater impact on the desired behaviours in patients. They found that sending a generic reminder text about dental appointments had a lesser impact than sending messages that contained positive reinforcement. The positive reinforcement messages, such as 'we really don't want you to miss your appointment' and indirect suggestions such as 'our records suggest a link between people who miss check-ups and those requiring more serious dental treatment later on' led to fewer patients missing their check-ups.

It's an interesting concept. Whilst on the one hand we know that the content of any communication with parents obviously matters, it is perhaps the more nuanced and precise ways that we need to give more intricate thought to.

Durrington Research School go on to describe their own implementation of this – directly sending a text message to students themselves, as well as parents, who have poor attendance, explaining in the message why they do not want them to miss school.

An example they provide on their blog is: 'Really looking forward to seeing you in school today. Your fellow students who have an attendance of 96% or higher are really improving their chances of achieving well in their GCSEs.'

As a school, they set this up as a small trial, with a control and intervention group, monitoring attendance over two terms, with their early results suggesting a positive effect score of 0.4, suggesting the strategy could have had a positive impact on improving attendance.

As a theory, then, there is perhaps scope for this to be used effectively in schools. This is especially interesting given the relatively low-cost methods that can be used in ways that might positively influence student behaviour. Although there are, of course, considerations to be made regarding the ethics of influencing behaviour, it is certainly one area that pastoral leaders can look to implement as part of building and crafting achievement and culture.

Practical strategies

A differentiated approach

As outlined in this chapter, best practice lies in targeted support for students. One way to do this is to ensure that there is a consistent approach to each 'category' of attendance.

96%+: Students receive verbal praise from their form tutor. A text message is sent home to parents that both recognises their achievements and reinforces key messages: 'Well done on such excellent attendance so far this academic year. Good attendance really helps learning and performance. There's even a link between attendance and exam success! Keep up the great attendance – it will really impact your learning!'

90–95.9%: Within this group, the importance of noticing students' attendance or absence can have a real impact as a preventative measure to stop attendance decreasing. Get your list together of which students are in this group. For each student, identify a key adult and enlist their support in noticing any absences. Ensure staff have this conversation promptly, ideally immediately as they return to school, and ask the student, privately where possible, what help they need after their absence. The power of someone noticing and caring, coupled with the opportunity to access support, can help students settle back into school even after a brief absence.

90–85%: This is beginning to get into really worrying territory. This is the level at which there needs to be a 1:1 approach with the student and their family. The aim here is to prevent further decline and increase the days that students attend. This is the kind of situation where you need weekly and half termly goals, a close working relationship, and open channels of communication between home and school. It's also the case that you need an honest relationship with home, whereby the family feel they can tell you if they are struggling to get a child to attend, rather than covering up a difficulty so as not to feel judged.

Below 85%: Hold an attendance panel. This is where you need a formal meeting with the family, the school, and external agencies. This will vary hugely depending on your school and your location. It may include staff from the LEA or other supporting agencies. It may also be an appropriate time to consider opening an Early Help if this isn't already in place.

Making attendance tangible

Students need clarity over what attendance figures equate to – 95% can sound excellent to students' parents. If you scored 95% in a test, you'd more than likely be pretty happy with yourself! Attendance doesn't work like this, but students and their families are not blessed with the expert knowledge of how assessment data builds in the same way that school staff are. Make sure that you regularly communicate how this translates to lost learning and days off school. The infographic below can be helpful. It's what I use regularly when discussing attendance concerns.

TABLE 1

Number of days' absence	Equals attendance one school year
9.5 days	95%
19 days	90%
28.5 days	85%
38 days	80%
47.5 days	75%
57 days	70%
66.5 days	65%

TABLE 2

Number of days' absence	Attendance over past six weeks
2 days	93%
3 days	90%
5 days	83%
8 days	73%
10 days	67%
15 days	50%

Strategic planning around special events

This is an interesting one, and one that is easily missed in the busy humdrum of the school calendar. Spend some time looking for specific patterns in your cohort's attendance, and perhaps even in the whole school. You may notice some patterns. For example, Fridays before a bank holiday weekend, the Monday after a half term, the last day of term, non-uniform day, Christmas jumper day. Once you have noticed a pattern, the next step is proactive planning; there's no point identifying a pattern without then trying to do something to prevent it forming in the future. I once trialled a 'special' year group football match, knowing that there was a pattern within a large peer group where attendance often dipped at the ends of half terms. In a group of 24 students, 23 of them attended school that day – primarily because they felt that they had an important contribution to make to their peer group in the form of the football match. Within that peer group, attendance improved when compared with previous figures for the end of a term. Furthermore, there were also interesting patterns in the year group. The match had become an event, a thing for people to attend. There was a social factor to it and attendance elsewhere within the year group also increased, albeit somewhat unexpectedly.

Sometimes attendance is about getting creative and trying different ideas, thinking outside the box, but also about knowing what is likely to motivate your students. By looking at patterns in data, you can start to think more strategically as a leader about how you might prevent problems before they arise.

Community links

Working with your community as a school can have real payoff, especially in terms of attendance. There will be local employers or local providers who have influential and important roles in your community. Make links with them and get them on board to support their community. For example, in my local area, there is a particular post 16 provider with whom places are highly sought after and that many students aspire to. By engaging them in school, and inviting them in, we're able to get them to talk to students about attendance and the importance it has in their future. This can be done as assemblies or more targeted work with vulnerable students. The old adage says it takes a village to raise a child – make use of yours, and enlist support from those people that students, and their families, know and respect.

Case study/Key learning review/Page to practise

Louisa is a new head of year. She picks up a year group at the beginning of year 9. She doesn't know that much about them as a year group. She's a maths teacher and hasn't taught many of them. She knows that attendance is important and plans to review it at October half term. In the first three weeks of the academic term, she can see some students have low attendance figures. She decides she will focus on them. After another four weeks, their attendance is much better. At the end of this half term, she reviews the individual attendance figures – there are at least 15 students who are now emerging as a concern.

Note down

Where do you think Louisa has gone wrong?

What might be the issue with the September data?

What could she have used that might give her a better insight?

What data should she be getting and when?

After the October half term, Louisa then compared her half term 1 data with the historical attendance data from the previous academic year. Doing this, she can see that it is similar students emerging as attendance concerns. She meets with each student individually and speaks to them about their attendance. Some of them are on 95.5%; others are as low as 67.3%.

Note down

Where is Louisa going wrong here?

How might she group students more effectively?

What strategies could she be using at this point that might help?

What advice would you give her if, as a more experienced pastoral leader, you were supporting her?

What should she prioritise over the next two academic terms to get a better handle on attendance?

Key Learning Points

1. Attendance is both important and messy.

2. There are several barriers to consider: academic, parental, health, bullying/peer relationships, socio-economic.

3. There are no silver bullets. It's about working with students, parents, staff, and external agencies to broker the best support for individuals.

4. Generally speaking, attendance categories are 96% and above, 90–95.9%, 95–89.9%, below 85%. Treat these differently and according to need.

5. Your role as a pastoral leader can be summarised as: data monitoring, first day contact, know and notice your students, involve parents, target support, positive reintegration.

6. Rewards and incentives need careful consideration. They may not help improve attendance.

7. Nudge Theory provides some interesting inspiration for innovative approaches to improving attendance.

RECOMMENDED READING

The Education Endowment Foundation (EEF) guidance report published in 2019 explores the evidence around how best we can work with parents effectively. Improving attendance is one area where our working relationships with parents are an instrumental part of any potential success. In the report, which is a must read, they make four main recommendations:

1. Critically review how you work with parents.
2. Provide practical strategies to support learning at home.
3. Tailor communications to encourage positive dialogue about learning.
4. Offer more sustained and intensive support where needed.

The report itself expands upon these core aspects in much more detail. It is an important document for any middle leader, pastoral or otherwise, to be well acquainted with.

What Works Clearinghouse are a US-based project with a team of 300 people from 6 organisations including the Institute of Education Sciences (IES), who aim to be a 'central and trusted source of scientific evidence for what works in education'. In essence, this is a similar model to the UK's EEF.

They have produced one of the most in-depth, evidence informed reviews around school attendance and school 'dropout'. Although written with a US context in mind, there are several important takeaways from their document Preventing Dropout in Secondary Schools.

Their four key recommendations for schools are to:

1. Monitor the progress of all students, and proactively intervene when students show early signs of attendance, behaviour, or academic problems.
2. Provide intensive, individualised support to students who have fallen off track and face significant challenges to success.

3. Engage students by offering curricula and programmes that connect schoolwork with college and career success and that improve students' capacity to manage challenges in and out of school.

4. For schools with many at-risk students, create small, personalised communities to facilitate monitoring and support.

A lengthy document, coming in at over 100 pages, it is a treasure trove of evidence informed inspiration and ideas for strategies to use in school. It is an absolute must read!

REFERENCES

Ariely, D. (2008). *Predictably Irrational: The hidden forces that shape our decisions.* New York, NY: Harper Collins.

Bettinger, E. and Slonim, R. (2007). Patience among Children, *Journal of Public Economics*, 19, pp. 343–363.

Cialdini, R.B. (2009). *Influence: Science and practice.* Fifth Edition. London: Pearson.

Damgaard, M.T. and Nielsen, H.S. (2018). Nudging in education, *Economics of Education Review*, 64, pp. 313–342.

Durrington Research School (2018). *An evidence informed approach to improving attendance.* Available at: https://researchschool.org.uk/durrington/news/an-evidence-informed-approach-to-improving-attendance. Accessed 26 July 2021.

Education Endowment Foundation (2019). *How Can Schools Support Parents' Engagement in their Children's Learning? Evidence from research and practice.* Available at: https://educationendowmentfoundation.org.uk/news/review-of-evidence-on-parental-engagement. Accessed 26 July 2021.

Kahneman, D. (2011). *Thinking, Fast and Slow.* New York, NY: Farrar, Straus and Giroux.

Robinson, D., Gallus, J., Lee, M.G. and Rogers, T. (2018). *The Demotivating Effect (and Unintended Message) of Awards.* HKS Faculty Research Working Paper Series RWP18-020.

Rumberger, R., Addie, H., Allensworth, E., Balfanz, R., Bruch, J., Dillon, E., Duardo, D., Dynarski, M., Furgeson, J., Jayanthi, M., Newman-Gonchar, R., Place, K. and Tuttle, C. (2017). Preventing Dropout in Secondary Schools (NCEE 2017-4028). Washington DC: National Center for Education Evaluation and Regional Assistance (NCEE), Institute of Education Science, U.S. Department of Education. Available at: https://whatworks.ed.gov. Accessed 22 January 2022.

Thaler, R. and Sunstein, C. (2008). *Nudge: Improving decisions about health, wealth, and happiness.* New Haven, CT & London: Yale University Press.

CHAPTER 6
WORKING WITH PARENTS

Meeting with parents is something that will take up a lot of your time as a pastoral leader. It is something you will do daily, often multiple times a day. It is also one of the most powerful weapons in your arsenal as a pastoral leader. Building, crafting, and nurturing these relationships is vital – it is often the key to making real improvements with students in school.

The evidence around this is also positive, suggesting repeatedly that parental engagement is one of the most important facets in improving outcomes for students. As well as being one of the most important strands, it is also one of the most difficult, frustrating, and challenging aspects of the job. Some parents can be very difficult to work with; others are a dream. It is often the more challenging ones with which your time and effort need to be most invested, alongside those who are more disengaged, even absent, from the child's education provision altogether.

Desforges and Abouchaar (2003, p. 87) summarise this well, stating that 'research consistently shows that what parents do with their children at home through the age range is much more significant than any other factor open to educational influence'.

They go on to elaborate one of the more pertinent points for secondary school professionals, exploring the fact that evidence repeatedly also seems to suggest that parental engagement often diminishes as a child progresses through their education. This pattern is often clear in secondary schools, where engagement in lower school is often more prevalent than that at Key Stage 4.

If you are working within Key Stage 4, where I have spent most of my career, you will be familiar with the narrative that at this age students should be responsible for themselves. Even the most well-meaning parents fall into this trap. Rather than leaving students to flounder at an age where they will be experiencing the first real high-stakes assessment of their lives, I would argue that the opposite is the case. We need parents and families to play an assertive role at home. If you are working within lower school, at Key Stage 3 one of the most important things to build is parental engagement throughout your key stage, and to lay the foundations for this engagement to continue into Key Stage 4.

Goodall and Vorhaus (2011) elaborate upon this, stating that:

> The more parents are engaged in the education of their children, the more likely their children are to succeed in the education system. School improvement and school effectiveness research consistently shows that parental engagement is one of the key factors in securing higher student achievement. Schools that improve and sustain improvement engage the communication and build strong links with parents. (p. 16)

Clearly, then, it is never more important that this engagement be present in Key Stage 4, when students are working towards their GCSEs. Such high-stakes assessments open, and sadly close, doors to students' future aspirations. As the stakes increase with time, so too should parental engagement. As a pastoral leader, communicating this to parents is vital – it is a message that needs to be shared regularly.

Goodall and Vorhaus (2011) also focus on what it is that makes a difference. Whilst they expand upon the likelihood of engagement being linked to social class, ethnicity, maternal educational levels, and material deprivation, they go on to show that even when these factors are accounted for, engagement continues to have a positive effect (Desforges and Abouchaar 2003).

This suggests, then, that the factor that makes a difference is *what parents do with their children*, rather than who they are or their life circumstances.

Engaging parents in this, and equipping them with this knowledge, is vital. It is, I would argue, one of the lead roles of a pastoral leader. You are uniquely positioned to ensure that parents know this, but also to act as their support in knowing what to do to make that crucial difference.

A uniting factor between parents and school staff lies in our wishes – we all want their child to succeed. As a pastoral leader, making sure that parents know what they need to be doing is vital. This can be easily overlooked in our profession – it can seem obvious to us what needs to happen in the home. It isn't always obvious, though, to busy parents, often with multiple children in the home, with busy lives, busy jobs, and the stresses of life all competing for limited attention. Rather than making assumptions, we should be playing a lead role in sharing strategies with parents so that they can act in the best interests of their child.

So what is it, then, that we need to be focussing on with parents?

Desforges and Abouchaar (2003) suggest that parents can have the most impact when they:

- Continue to take an interest in students' aspirations and their education.
- Discuss current affairs, films, and books.
- Encourage and support their homework – crucially, supporting them to do it rather than helping them with it. A big, important distinction.
- Have activities in the home that promote independence, time management, and critical thinking skills.

One of the key aspects of this lies in supporting parents' ability to conduct the above activities in the home. One barrier that you will have undoubtedly come across is parents feeling inadequate when dealing with students' academic work.

Education changes over time; I know myself that I often see what students are doing in GCSE subjects I studied, and it can seem a world away from what we knew during our time at school.

Parents have a similar experience, especially if they feel that their own academic achievements were not significant. It is vital, then, that we play a role in managing this. Parents need to know they are not expected to be subject experts – their role isn't in helping students academically. That's what teachers are for.

Rather, their role is creating a home environment where students engage in academic work, homework, and revision.

A further facet within this lies in ensuring parents know what to do when their child experiences an academic barrier. Rather than feeling helpless if they can't help, instead they need to know what to do in this position. School systems may be clear to us, but to parents working at a distance from our institutions, the processes for getting and receiving help can seem overwhelming. Make sure parents know what to do in this position, rather than students simply giving up.

There should be a system by which students can access help, either using a VLE/digital learning system that may be in place in school or by communicating their difficulties with their teachers. It is also important that we recognise that doing this can itself be a barrier. I have worked with many parents over the years who lack the confidence to contact a teacher. Picking up the phone or writing an email to someone they don't know well can seem overwhelming. In this case, I often tell parents to use me as their primary point of contact – if we have an approachable relationship with them, this is a perfect opportunity to develop that, and to show that we act quickly, thus building up trust in us as a school. Simply arranging for the child to get some help with an academic barrier can make a huge difference and serve to support the parent in the home. Further to this, Harris and Goodall (2007) detail that it is this genuine interest and support that students themselves value the most, rather than more high-profile events and activities such as responding to school correspondence and attendance at parents' evenings. The more students, and their families, value school, the more they will positively engage in all it has to offer.

Taking a proactive role in supporting this is crucial in our collective endeavour to ensure our students secure the very best outcomes that they can in their time with us.

It is interesting, then, what the research suggests about parental involvement; it is the support rather than the in-school actions that make the difference. As a pastoral leader, it can be easy to judge this by parents' involvement in school life – being present in school activities, being a school governor, attending parents' evening.

These appear to be poor proxies for measuring parental engagement – indeed, the linguistic distinction is important. Engagement is that which supports and shows an interest; involvement is that which is activity-based in school.

Goodall and Montgomery (2014) state that:

> Engagement with children's learning may not equate to – and should not be judged on the basis of – [involvement] with the school. Many parents – particularly those from ethnic minorities or those facing economic challenge, find [involvement] with schools difficult, but still have a strong desire to be involved in their children's learning and education. (p. 400)

Put simply, we must ensure that we do not fall for these proxies – the result will inevitably be that our efforts and time, precious as our time is, are focussed in the wrong areas. Given how time intensive our roles are, and how much demand our time is subjected to, we have a responsibility to ensure that we use that time for only those things that will make a real impact. The evidence, then, gives us the best bets on our time. Put simply, this should be used to target parents' knowledge of what to do in the home that makes a difference, and in supporting them to do this effectively.

The role of the pastoral leader in removing barriers to engagement cannot be overestimated. Whilst some of these barriers can be practical – such as ensuring we can meet their needs at times that work for them and in being flexible around their demanding lives – as we know, these are poor reflections of engagement, despite being important factors in parents' feelings and involvement in school.

In short, these are the exact kinds of adaptations we should make, but we shouldn't simply pat ourselves on the back at this point. In their 2011 study of 47 schools, OFSTED concluded that when it comes to successful parental engagement:

Schools that were the most successful in relating to all parents believed that no parent was unreachable. They were very persistent when they needed to be. Sensitive telephone calls, visits to homes or meetings held at neutral non-threatening locations, such as community centres or supermarkets, often helped to make positive connection.

It is this tenacity, this drive to do the hard work that changes lives, that can be best driven by pastoral leaders. It comes from the desire to remove any and all barriers, because we know the value that doing so has: it changes lives. These barriers are harder to overcome, and often are psychological in nature from parents. There are no silver bullets with this; research doesn't have all the answers, mainly because these deeply personal barriers differ hugely between people. We are human and complex. One of the most rewarding aspects of the job is cracking this nut – taking a difficult and challenging barrier and giving your all to remove it. This work is a privilege; parents make themselves vulnerable and we must give this the respect it deserves. It can be hard for anyone to make themselves vulnerable, but doing so for the betterment of your child is one of the most special moments in a parent–school relationship.

Dealing with difficulties

Despite the importance of nurturing these vital relationships, they are rarely straightforward. One of the most difficult aspects of our role lies in those difficult conversations we have with parents, especially where we need to contact home because something has gone wrong in school.

It is also one of the areas of the job where there can be a real dearth of training – it is too often simply assumed that we know how to have these difficult conversations, when, especially at the early stages of our career, we don't.

In the early stages of my career, one of the most important opportunities for me was in working as an assistant head of year. This submersed me in the role, but also allowed me to learn the ropes, to observe the difficult conversations, and to dissect strategies for this with a more experienced colleague leading the way. It was a vital, formative step. As funding pressures in schools have increased, roles and opportunities such as this have increasingly diminished. It is entirely possible in today's world to become a pastoral leader without any of these formative and developmental opportunities, and suddenly you're expected simply to know how to navigate this challenging world. It felt important to me, then, to explore this in more detail in this book, and to share what I have learnt in the hopes that it helps those of you who may find yourselves in this position.

The difficult call home

It may be that you know already that you're headed for a difficult conversation. On other occasions, it may take you completely by surprise. In either situation, the planning remains the same. I would always prepare for any conversation as though it were a difficult one; if it turns out to be much simpler, it's always a welcome surprise in your day.

I would begin any call by introducing myself and using my first name rather than 'Miss Forrester'. This immediately helps break down any power dynamics – it puts you on a level with parents where that imbalance feels more removed. Equally, always look up a parent's legal name on your information management system such as SIMs. That way you avoid any awkward name issues. I would open the conversation by asking for the parent first, so something along the lines of: 'Good morning, please could I speak to Mrs Jones?'

At this point, once you've verified you are speaking to the right person, I would follow up with: 'It's Amy Forrester, James's head of year from school.'

I would then follow by checking that it is a good time to speak – you never know when a call is landing in someone else's day, and the last thing you want to do is proceed when it is not a good time – 'Do you have five minutes for a quick chat?' or 'Is now a good time to have a quick chat?' This way, you're offering an 'out' if it isn't, but also showing that you value their time and input.

Once you've established this, I always try to start with some positives. Jumping straight into a negative can immediately turn the tone of the conversation. Something along the lines of: 'James has been doing really well recently and I've noticed in particular that he's been working well in maths whenever I've popped into lessons.' By using a positive, and making a direct reference, you're showing that you know the child and have recognised there is more to them than the incident you're phoning about.

I would then follow this with something like: 'Unfortunately, he's not managed to show that excellent side of himself at break time today.' By phrasing it in this way, you're acknowledging implicitly that you know the lovely side to the child. The parent can then feel as though you know their child well and that you are viewing them as a whole person, acknowledging the things they know to be true about their child.

At this point, it's important to be clear and emotionless and to seek not to apportion blame. Outline actions and specific behaviours that the child has shown, such as: 'Unfortunately, at break time today, he told another child to F off.'

When it comes to retelling incidents to parents, I always feel it is important to use the exact wording a child has used. You can acknowledge that you're forced to use their words and that they are unpleasant, but it is important to use them. It keeps things clear.

At this point, you may find a parent has lots of questions – and your ability to answer them will depend on a number of factors. It is absolutely fine to say that you need to spend more time investigating, or to speak to other witnesses. The reason you're calling is to make the parent aware, and, crucially, to enlist their support. This part of the conversation is key. Make sure you're clear on this before you head into the call. Do you need them to speak to the child to find out more information? Do you need them to support your sanction? Do you need them to back the support you're putting in place as a school?

By being clear with what you need, you're establishing the importance of working together, and it is vital that the parent knows this in the interaction. Stress this point – that you want to work together to avoid problems in the future. You both have common ground in that you care about the child and want them to be successful in school. You also have high expectations, and that is also how you show that you care about a child. There needs to be a united front if things are going to improve in school, and you need to be clear about this with parents.

It is rare, in my experience, that a parent won't see the importance of this. It can also help at this stage to enlist their advice as well – they know their child far better than you do. Give them the opportunity to share this with you – ask what, in their view, you need to factor in. This is not about making excuses; rather, it is about ensuring your response is well matched to the child. For example, it may be that the parent knows their child is unlikely to open up if there is a problem. You need to know that and find a way forward where there is a mechanism for this, so that you can be proactive in future and prevent situations from escalating. Working together with a parent to find this way forward is the aim in this part of the conversation.

At the end of the call, make time to thank them for their time and support. Where there are particularly fractious relationships between the school and the family, it is always good practice to follow up the call with an email summarising the conversation. This also helps ensure you have accurate records should you need them in future. Record-keeping is a huge part of the job. Ensuring there are records of all communications done over the phone is really important. If this isn't yet your school policy, create yourself a phone log sheet per call. Store them electronically either in email folders or electronic safeguarding software so that you are able to easily recap on previous communications with parents. Future you will always thank past you for this!

You should also follow up with further thanks, if and when the parent shows their support. It's easy sometimes to forget these opportunities in a busy pastoral leader's day. A quick email, text, or call can go a long way in developing a relationship and showing the parent that you're noticing positives as well as negatives. This nurturing approach to relationships can help next time you need to make a call – the parent can see that you've been true to your word, that you've done what you said you'd do, and worked supportively with them. A wise pastoral leader, Ian Routledge, once said to me that this is where you 'earn your keep' as a head of year – the small moments that no one notices or sees, but that are vital in creating a good culture of openness and support with the parents you work with. It's the call you make at 6 p.m. to keep them informed, or the email you send at the end of the day, as you promised, that really matters in this job. What matters is that the parent, and to a certain extent the child, knows that you, and therefore the school, are working with them as parents. It's the human side of the job – this must never be overlooked.

When calls go wrong

There may, of course, be interactions that you have that cross the line of acceptable communication. You might find yourself being sworn at or shouted at on the call. This is not acceptable behaviour and you need to very quickly inform the parent on the call that this is not acceptable, and that you will terminate the call if they continue. If they do continue, terminate the call, make a clear record of the conversation, and enlist your line manager at this point. No one is expected to put up with abuse whilst in their place of work. A good school should have a policy around parental communications and have steps for dealing with this that your line manager will support you with.

It is important, however, in our role, to maintain personal responsibility and involvement with the child. This is especially true when there are phone calls that are rude rather than abusive. It can be tempting to pass these on, but I would always advocate 'picking up your own tab' in this respect. By all means, discuss these with your line manager. Work together on strategies to improve the relationship and ensure you are well supported. But your role is not one where you can shirk responsibility for these difficult moments. In time, you'll come to find the challenge enjoyable. There is no greater feeling than tenaciously persevering with communication and getting to a better position with a family.

Practical strategies for engaging parents

Methods of communication

Making communication easy is a vital part of the job. Traditionally the realm of phone calls, schools are increasingly using digital communications such as email as their primary method of communication. Making use of a pastoral smartphone for work purposes can really help. During the pandemic, we made this available to parents, both with calls and as a number to text or use on a platform such as WhatsApp. We did have some reservations about this, but it was a game-changing strategy for us. It made contact with some families much easier – it is often a method they feel comfortable using, and, as such, we saw vastly improved communication with families that had previously been harder to reach. It is a strategy that we have continued with, such was its success. Support staff such as our attendance officer, and pastoral admin staff, also had access to a smartphone, and this has been instrumental in their roles too.

Supporting learning

In a previous chapter, I wrote about the introduction of parent information evenings in which key knowledge around revision and homework was shared. This same information is crucial in building parental engagement, and sharing important messages around this theme can really empower parents to do the right things at home. Make use of messaging systems in school to send regular 'nudges' (see Nudge Theory, Chapter 5), such as 'Recapping learning regularly can help retain learning over a longer period of time.' 'Helping your child to recap learning regularly is a great way to help support them at home. When they get home tonight, put some time aside to quiz them on their learning – simply talking about it is a great recap. You don't need to be a subject expert; ask them to explain it to you!' Sending short strategies such as this, on a regular basis, can really help, especially in busy households where things like this can fall to the bottom of the priority list.

Parent feedback

Getting parental feedback on school systems and provision can be an excellent way of informing your actions as a head of year. Each half term, I would always try to find time to make some proactive calls home simply to talk to parents about school and anything we might be able to do better. I try to choose families where there hasn't been any contact in the previous half term.

I tend to ask questions such as:

- How are they getting on with their schoolwork?
- How much homework are they getting?
- What are you doing at home that's working well with them?
- Are there any issues or concerns you don't know what to do about?
- What are some of the things you think we could be a bit better at as a school?

This open and honest conversation can be really enlightening, and it helps you get a flavour for how the actions and provisions in a school are translating on the ground. It's also an opportunity to resolve any niggles that parents might have had but did not necessarily share with you. It shows an outward-facing school keen to work with its families and community.

Positive recognition

There are always students who are at risk of getting lost in the system. They're often students who work hard day in, day out. They hand in all their work on time. Their behaviour is excellent. Their name rarely comes across your desk in any sort of negative way. These students need acknowledgement, and who better than their head of year to do that? Students like this very easily fall through the net and we do need to take regular opportunities to remind ourselves of this and notice them.

I also use reports as a great opportunity to do this. Sending a quick email to 20 parents to celebrate their achievements and consistency is a lovely way of establishing communication with parents. Whenever I do this, I learn something about a child – either something we've been unaware of or something about a child's character and behaviour that I hadn't considered. It's a win–win strategy.

Case study

Alice is head of year 9. She has a cohort of around 25 families who she feels are not engaged in their child's education. Any contact she has had with them has been apathetic – there has been little interest in talking about the child's education and aspirations. She wants to focus on these families and try to get them more engaged.

Note down:

Where should she start with this?

What might be some of the reasons for the parents not being engaged?

What strategies could she use to try to increase their engagement?

What could she ask them to do at home to support their child's learning?

How might she best sustain this over time?

How might she prepare for calling home, especially where some of the parents can be difficult on the phone?

Why is her time well spent?

Key Learning Points

- Parental engagement can have a significant impact on outcomes.
- The evidence is much less conclusive around how best to engage parents.
- Your role as a pastoral leader is perfectly positioned to do some high-impact work on this.
- Don't confuse involvement with engagement – they are not the same.
- The most important thing that parents can do is to support education and aspirations from home and create the best conditions for learning.

RECOMMENDED READING

The Education Endowment Foundation (EEF) study into the evidence around how schools can support parents' engagement is an excellent guidance document that can be found on their website at: https:// educationendowmentfoundation.org.uk/school-themes/parental-engagement/. It covers four core recommendations and is full of inspiration for improving your provision as a school.

United Learning, a leading multi-academy trust, have produced an excellent, comprehensive document exploring parental engagement and whole school strategies. An excellent read with some really interesting case studies from their own schools within the trust: https://unitedlearning. org.uk/united-thinking/articles/effective-parental-engagement.

REFERENCES

Desforges, C. and Abouchaar, A. (2003). *The Impact of Parental Involvement, Parental Support and Family Education on Pupil Achievement and Adjustment: A literature review.* London. Department for Education and Skills.

Goodall, J. and Montgomery, C. (2014). Parental Involvement to Parental Engagement: A continuum, *Educational Review*, 46, pp. 399–410.

Goodall, J. and Vorhaus, J. (2011). *Review of Best Practice in Parental Engagement*. London: Department for Education.

Harris, A. and Goodall, J. (2007). *Engaging Parents in Raising Achievement: Do parents know they matter?* London: Department for Children, Schools and Families.

OFSTED (2011). *Schools and Parents*. Available at: https://assets. publishing.service.gov.uk/government/uploads/system/uploads/ attachment_data/file/413696/Schools_and_parents.pdf. Accessed 2 August 2021.

CHAPTER 7

PASTORAL LEADERSHIP AND MANAGEMENT

When we think about leadership in schools, we often rightly focus first on what this means. Louis et. al. (2010), in their comprehensive review into educational leadership, focus on the core functions of school leadership: setting direction and exercising influence. Ensuring that school improvement is at the heart of what every leader's role in school is forms the foundations of any successful school.

As a pastoral leader, it is easy to feel that the importance and coverage of our area of expertise is too often overlooked. What is true, though, is that anything relating to leadership as an aspect of school life pertains to us as pastoral leaders. I'd go so far as to say that we have the most important role in this; without us, nothing else can happen. The energy and focus invested into leading on teaching and learning will not have the impact desired if pastoral leaders aren't effective in their role. We keep all the cogs turning in ways that people rarely see or appreciate.

This is acknowledged, often implicitly, in models of leadership. If we took at Hallinger and Heck (2011), for example, they present school leadership as that which influences the learning outcomes of students through three main variables: school culture; academic structures and processes; and people.

Within this, then, pastoral care has a significant role. We are often the people on the front line of a school culture; we are immersed in the student experience of our school. What a policy or laminate says about culture and what we live and breathe can be worlds apart.

Our understanding of the school culture is more likely to be the most accurate. We know the reality of our schools, and what culture our students experience daily. We're in the best position to set a culture, and to uphold it too – I've touched on that in Chapter 2. However, when a school structure is examined, it's easy to forget this. Attention too often falls mostly at the door of academic middle leaders. Pastoral leaders must be at the forefront of any model of school leadership. Hallinger and Heck acknowledge that leadership is also about people. Pastoral leaders, I would say, manage and lead far more people than do academic middle leaders. Whilst we lead our pastoral teams of school staff, we also lead our students in a far more visible way than do other middle leaders. We also have, I would suggest, far more communication with parents and our wider community – again, more people.

Our actions have wide-reaching consequences, and we are often the face of the school. We're the people parents know. We're the people students know. We're the people employers know. Our actions, then, and our leadership, are far more visible, and have a wider reaching impact on the way our stakeholders feel about our school. Rightly or wrongly, parents may base their view of the school on their interactions with us. Therefore, what we do matters; we want to reflect the excellence of our school.

There is, thankfully, an increasing leadership focus on pastoral care – we can see already that what unites us – our students' wellbeing and success in school – is central in pastoral leadership. The definition of pastoral leadership, however, is perhaps more complex than that of generic school leadership. It can mean many different things to many different people; it is, if nothing else, a broad church.

We see this reflected in academic literature and research around pastoral leadership, with various explorations of pastoral leadership reflecting this wide range of views.

Purdy (2013) embraces this broad nature of pastoral leadership, stating that it is 'much more than an emotional crutch' (p. 2), going on to state that it is about a whole school atmosphere that ensures young people are prepared for the realities of life and the inevitable challenges that lie ahead. Grove

(2004, p. 34), however, has perhaps a more aspirational view of pastoral leadership, commenting that it is 'all measures to assist an individual person or a community to reach their full potential, success and happiness in coming to a deeper understanding of their own humanness'. This mixed picture and range of views is not uncommon in education; philosophies and ideologies vary and run deep in schools, among teachers, and within society as a whole. This is why, I would argue, you need to work in a school whose vision and philosophy are similar to yours. Whilst it is important to interrogate and challenge your own views as a professional, being on the same page as your school and its senior leaders is really important. You should live and breathe your values; they are what motivates you in the role of pastoral leader and in the work you do with students and their families.

Leadership is not just about our parents and our communities, though. It is also about the teachers we lead and the environment our teachers are working in. We must never overlook this. We are part of the staff body, and pastoral leadership is not solely about leading students; it is also about leading staff – something that can be forgotten all too easily.

Cardno (2012) and Louis et al. (2010) acknowledge this in their work, focussing on the notion that leaders shape this environment in which teachers work. This is one of the most powerful aspects of pastoral care. Whilst our primary role lies in supporting students, we also exist to support staff. Our role, I would suggest, is best encapsulated as supporting students so that teachers can do their job to the best of their ability. We have huge influence on our students' behaviour and attitudes in school. One wrong move can easily undermine a class teacher's professionalism. We must, therefore, have this at the heart of our leadership – we seek to serve teachers' needs as much as we serve our students' needs. Both are crucial in achieving the very best for our students' learning outcomes.

We also have specific areas of leadership within our pastoral teams, often having responsibility for a team of form tutors. This is where we have the most on-the-ground leadership – this is how we create our pastoral team, our vision, and our success.

It can also be one of the most difficult areas. We generally aren't line managers of tutors. We have limited time with them. In busy teachers' lives, we can also fall to the bottom of the list. This isn't to apportion blame to form tutors – their teaching lives are frantic. If you're a non-teaching head of year, it can be hard to empathise with this, but I would say that this always needs to be in your mind. I have found I have most success when I take this into account and keep the demands on teachers' time minimal, so that the time they do have can be kept for what is most important – working with our students.

On the ground, for me, this means ensuring that much of your pastoral provision is planned for tutors. By all means, provide them with time and support to have some ownership and create their own resources and ideas. Some of your tutors will excel at this. But you also need to consider that others may not. The best way to manage this, in my experience, lies in centralising resources – where you have tutors who are keen to develop and contribute, include their work in this, and share this widely around your team. But I also ensure that there are sufficient resources in place for tutors to use that require minimal time in advance, so that all the time you have available within your pastoral provision is used wisely.

I believe that every second matters in a school. We have limited time, in the grand scheme of things, with our students. We owe it to them to ensure that we make the absolute most of this. The worst thing, for me, is to have that awful 'dead time' within pastoral provision, where students are sitting around and talking. They can do that at break, or at lunch, or in their own time. We should not be using our time in school to give them more of this. Making this clear to your tutor team, and clearly setting out your vision, is vital.

So, too, is ensuring that your team are well supported to bring this vision to fruition.

Crucial within this is what research tells us about empowering teachers to find their workplace a positive and meaningful place. Leithwood (2007) found that teachers finding their work meaningful, the encouragement of collaboration, clear and morally inspiring goals, and collegiality are all features of a school leadership culture that have a positive impact on teachers' lives.

Again, it's clear to see where pastoral leadership plays an effective role in this. Our work is morally inspiring – we work with students as individuals, in a holistic sense, playing a significant role both when their lives are going well and when they face the sometimes harrowing and distressing events that all too often plague our young people.

Form tutors have a huge role within this, and enacting this, empowering your team to be able to take a leading role in the lives of our young people, is vital. Nurturing these trusting relationships, where form tutors are trusted and empowered to do this, is also a common feature emphasised in the research around school leadership (Hayes, Christy, Mills and Lingard 2004; Leithwood et al. 2010; Tamati 2011).

Dufour and Marzano (2011) expand upon this, exploring the idea that it is this moral purpose that the best leaders place at the heart of what they do. In what is perhaps the most poetically beautiful definition of leadership, they state that leadership is 'an affair of the heart' (p. 1). Certainly, in working with a range of highly effective and experienced pastoral leaders, anecdotally at least, this is what ties them together as highly effective in their roles. They see this – the uniting power of the heart – and live this value in all that they do, with students, with staff, with parents. It is, in my experience, one of the most powerful aspects of leading others. Finding what unites us and brings us together, and what motivates us as individuals, is crucial in any leadership role. In pastoral leadership, then, maintaining this core focus on our students and their lives is vital. What else unites us if it is not to change lives?

Increasingly, in more recent times, we have seen the development of the 'hero model' of leadership. This term encapsulates the increasing focus on personal attributes, often generic, which are said by some to be the gold standard of school leadership.

Words such as 'inspiration' and 'visionary' are too often thrown around, featuring highly in the narrative around school leadership. Pastoral leadership is particularly vulnerable to this – too often we are seen as some mythical being, a hero who can deal with anything that occurs. In reality, we become a convenient dumping ground for issues that no one else has the time, expertise, or inclination to deal with. As a profession, pastoral leaders need to fight against this. It may seem counterproductive – we often revel in taking the most difficult issues and dealing with them. It's in our nature; it's why we are drawn to this professional niche. However, we are, as a professional group, better than this. We cannot allow ourselves to become this metaphorical dumping ground. In many ways, our fight lies in the way pastoral leadership is spoken about and in the way we define what excellence looks like when we talk about pastoral leadership.

Domain-based leadership vs skills-based leadership

The 'hero model' is not something unique to pastoral leadership. It appears in all aspects of school leadership. Indeed, as Lock (2020) explores in *The researchED Guide to Leadership: An evidence-informed guide for teachers*, 'the hero paradigm of school leadership is a manifestation of generic leadership' (p. 12). It is on this genericism, then – the catch-all adjectives of 'inspirational' and 'outstanding' – that we need to focus ourselves further. But not, perhaps, in the way you might expect.

Lock goes on to suggest that such 'vague notions of generic leadership are unhelpful when it comes to leading schools' (p. 13). This is a concept worth exploring in the pursuit of excellence in school leadership of pastoral care, as well as leadership in general. Lock argues that these generic approaches, with which he believes there are real problems, are deeply embedded and infinitely common within the educational leadership sphere. He gives the example of Steve Radcliffe's FED model of leadership: future, engage, deliver. This is one of many examples when you look across the leadership picture. The assumptions of models such as this, Lock argues, work alongside the assumption that approaches such as these can be applied to any institution – a hospital, a school, a bank. They are, in essence, a general model that some believe can be implemented regardless of what organisation or institution is being led.

Lock argues that underpinning these models are generic 'skills', skills which, he argues, are actually underpinned by domain specific knowledge. To the untrained eye, effective leaders display these skills in abundance. However, he argues that they are the product of excellent domain specific knowledge – that is, the knowledge of the area in which you lead.

Indeed, Lock goes on to outline a recent linguistic switch when it comes to the way leadership is spoken about. He gives the examples of phrases such as 'selflessness, integrity, objectivity, accountability, honesty' (p. 14), and the examples that describe leaders as people who should show 'the following personal characteristics or virtues: trust, wisdom, kindness, justice, service, courage and optimism' (p. 14).

It's hard not to see his point; these are all personal qualities that are, in fact, hard to define and even harder to pin down. They are traits that I'm sure many of us would like to see in ourselves as pastoral leaders. They are, however, a poor proxy for leadership; as Lock says, '[k]nowledge and experience of the domain of school leadership is a necessary ingredient of being an effective school leader, and it is probably a bigger ingredient than the orthodoxy has considered' (p. 15).

For pastoral leaders, this is particularly pertinent. There is a substance to what we do; we are far more than the adverbial generic descriptors. There is a vast knowledge base underpinning what we do. Much of this is learnt on the job. By its very nature, pastoral leadership is deeply unique – we may deal with similar problems, but they are then often varied by the context and the individual to which they apply.

In growing our experience as a pastoral leader, we build a knowledge base from which we develop our leadership. If you think, for a moment, of the best pastoral leaders you know – what is it that defines them as such?

For me, it is their wisdom. They know what to do when faced with a significant problem. They have a huge experience to draw from, and they use this to make the best decisions in a challenging situation. They always seem to know what to do. Indeed, this perhaps reflects Lock's argument. Their domain specific knowledge is strong.

Matthew Evans, an experienced and highly successful head teacher, also explores this concept in his book *Leaders with Substance: An antidote to genericism in schools* (2019).

In a similar vein to Lock (2020, p. 36), he argues that it is 'our schema of knowledge' that creates and defines the very best leaders, not the generic field of leadership. He goes on to argue that it is this relevant knowledge that allows them to best deal with the problems they encounter as school leaders.

This is central to the leadership life of a pastoral leader. In our role, we encounter problems regularly, sometimes, it feels, on a minute-by-minute basis on particularly challenging days! This high level of problem-solving isn't particularly unique, but it is one of the most demanding parts of our job. It is in our ability to deal with these problems, to lead the path through them, that our leadership really lives. It is fundamental, therefore, that we amass this knowledge into order to be successful pastoral leaders. That isn't to say we must be perfect; the thing I love and value most about pastoral leadership is the very fact that you are guaranteed to encounter new and diverse problems regularly. They will challenge you, both in your abilities and in your moral imperatives. It is a never a job in which you will reach a state of nirvana – your knowledge base will always develop. You will never have learnt it all.

It is this experience of dealing with problems, with new and unique challenges, that develops you as a pastoral leader. As with any leadership role, when you are new to it, you will undertake a strong learning curve. It is easy to feel intimidated by the job, to feel that there is so much to know that you will *never* know it all. That much is true – you'll never know all there is to know. But you will learn – you'll learn from colleagues, you'll learn from training, you'll learn from situations, you'll learn from experience. It is vital, though, that a key part of your professional practice is amassing this experience and drawing on it regularly. This is your domain specific knowledge, your 'schema of knowledge' in the job.

In Lock's book, there are chapters from several leading experts in the field of school leadership. It is a must read for all school leaders, such is the rich and diverse content it contains; it is gold dust. In Chapter 3, Jen Barker and Tom Rees explore a useful model for school leaders, one of which captures the vital role that domain specific knowledge underpins.

Their model contains the following concepts (p. 45):

1. Expertise
2. Mental models
3. Persistent problems
4. Knowledge

This model lends itself very well to domain specific pastoral leadership.

Expertise

Under expertise, they argue that expert school leaders are 'made, not born' (p. 47). Within pastoral care, this is a vital concept. All too often, we idolise pastoral leaders as being born for the job. I've said it myself enough times. I'm sure you can think of your own examples too. They're the kind that make it look easy when all of us know it is anything but.

Barker and Rees cite Bloom (1984, p. 48) when exploring the research that flies in the face of these assumptions, and in fact suggest that 'expert performance has little to do with innate talents or traits'. They go on to elaborate that this is, in part at least, because expertise is 'effortfully acquired' (Bereiter and Scardamalia 1993, p. 48).

In pastoral care, this expertise takes time to build. It is vital, especially in the early stages of your career, to acknowledge this. It can be the case that you are promoted into the role of pastoral leader, with precious little experience in the field. The metaphorical frying pan into the fire was made for us! I remember, in the early days of pastoral leadership, feeling entirely unqualified and frankly quite scared of the responsibility I suddenly had. I didn't have any of the answers. Suddenly, significant problems became my responsibility. It's a journey that most pastoral leaders have made – it is somewhat unique in this, I feel. Whilst that isn't to say that all new leaders feel this, in pastoral care it is a different beast. The pace, ferocity, and importance of the problems we encounter cannot be underestimated. It is at this stage that expertise needs to take priority – you must learn to lean on others, be they colleagues in other year groups or your DSL (designated safeguarding lead) or your line manager. Those with more experience have more expertise – do not be intimidated by this. You will become this yourself in time – but you must seek support in the early days whilst you build that expertise.

Mental models

Barker and Rees (2020, p. 49) argue that it is these mental models that we build through expertise that school leadership relies upon. They define these as 'representations people hold about the enormous range of things they do. They are underpinned by knowledge and developed through instruction, experience and significant amounts of practice and feedback'.

They argue that the benefits of these lie in being able to solve problems in less time or with less effort (Simon 1992) and improved pattern recognition (Kahneman and Klein 2009). Pattern recognition, they explain, enables leaders to 'spot where a problem is similar to one that has been dealt with previously or to recognise where a situation poses a novel challenge' (p. 49).

In thinking about pastoral care, then, this feels particularly relevant. Our roles are quite often dealing with similar issues, particularly when it comes to problems within school, or within a child's life. For example, it is highly likely that you will encounter friendship issues very regularly as a pastoral leader. You're also likely to have to deal with bullying, self-harm, eating disorders, and so on.

These examples also lend themselves well to pattern recognition. One could look like the other, for example, and it is with experience in dealing with these, in recognising the behaviours and warning signs, that you will begin to hone your pastoral skills to deal with things in the right way. In time, this pattern recognition also helps your efficiency, as Barker and Rees argue.

As you grow and build your domain specific knowledge, an issue that may take an entire day of your time will take a lot less. You learn a lot from each issue. For example, you'll learn in time that if a theft issue comes across your desk, you want to deal with that straight away, when you're likely to be able to find the item. Experience here teaches you that you're much more likely to get to the bottom of it on the day it happens, so if you're in the middle of a less time sensitive issue, you'll know to pick this up immediately. That is just one example; there are countless others that you will learn over the course of your pastoral leadership journey. It is these mental models that Barker and Rees argue will guide action. Crucial in this is the idea that they should *guide action*. As Barker and Rees argue, it is not simply the acquisition of knowledge that matters. It is the application of this in guiding our processes and actions that leads to a 'change in behaviour' which improves our leadership (p. 50).

An important part of this, as a pastoral leader, is taking the time to process and reflect on the things we deal with. We work at such a fast pace that it can be difficult to literally catch a breath in between the problems that come our way. Reflection can fall to the bottom of our priority list, but we must not allow this. It will, in time, hinder our development into effective pastoral leaders.

This reflection can be informal, simply thinking over your actions and reviewing what was effective and, crucially, what was not. In thinking about this, we must learn from our failures and mistakes as much as we learn about what went well. Our failures and mistakes are often the richest learning event for us. We endeavour to create cultures where our students do not fear failure; as pastoral leaders, we need to live that reality if we are truly to create conditions in which failure breeds success.

Reviewing and reflection are also an important part of line management; your relationship with your line manager should make time for this. There should be a collaborative, respectful opportunity for you to both examine how you've dealt with things and offer the opportunity to talk and learn from one another. It can be hard, especially when our role as pastoral leaders often feels like we need to have all the answers, to be able to be open and honest about our practice. It is imperative that we do; it is normal and human to make mistakes. But we should not be making the same mistake twice. Line management is the perfect opportunity to learn how to proactively avoid the same mistakes in future.

Persistent problems

Barker and Rees, acknowledging their term is borrowed from Mary Kennedy (2016), focus on 'understanding the persistent problems school leaders face [that can] help us to have a better understanding of the purpose of their work' (p. 49).

They go on to outline several persistent problems that school leaders face, acknowledging that context plays a large role in this: school culture, development, curriculum, behaviour, school improvement, administration, and self.

As pastoral leaders, our roles fall within a few categories – school culture, behaviour, school improvement. Within this, though, context also plays a significant role. They acknowledge that although behaviour is an overarching theme, this will present differently based on our roles, with that of a head of year being very different from other forms of school leadership (p. 49).

The phrase 'persistent problems' feels like a very pertinent phrase when it comes to pastoral leadership! We do inevitably face these persistent problems on a frustratingly regular basis. I'm sure you'll share that sentiment; we all have those 'not again!' moments where we occasionally might want to smash our head into a wall as a preferable alternative.

However, it is on these persistent problems that we might better focus our development. Indeed, as they are common in occurrence, our time must be impactful and well used. Barker and Rees argue that 'a comprehensive understanding of the problems leaders face, and the knowledge needed to solve them, means we can effectively structure and sequence the development of leaders'.

This is all about the way we use our domain specific knowledge in practice. To do so, 'we need to get an insight into the sophisticated knowledge that leaders will need' (p. 49). As a pastoral leader, it is these persistent issues where you need to take a proactive role too and take some personal responsibility for expanding your own knowledge and implementation of this in practice. This is a perfect opportunity for development as a leader, sharing these frustrations with colleagues and exploring what they do in similar situations. This unified approach is vital in pastoral teams; we're often dealing with the same problems, just with different year groups. Our approaches to these can be improved by sharing knowledge and expertise, working collaboratively to explore more effective responses to persistent problems.

Knowledge

In the final stage of their model, Barker and Rees suggest that 'expertise is predicated on knowledge'. They argue that there is a 'hidden knowledge' that sits beneath experts:

1. Informal knowledge: think of this as 'expert common sense' (Bereiter and Scardamalia 1993, p. 54), where you know to view CCTV before deciding on what you think happened.

2. Impressionistic: think of this as your impression of a situation, like knowing that you need to call a certain parent about a problem before the child gets home to share their inaccurate version!

3. Self-regulatory: think of this as how you manage yourself within the job – a more metacognitive process. Think of this as when you know you need to step away from your email response for 24 hours before you send it!

As we examine ourselves as pastoral leaders, these elements of 'hidden knowledge' provide a helpful framework for us as developing leaders because they allow us to think more explicitly about the types of knowledge we have and what we need to develop further. For example, it took me a good few years to develop my self-regulatory knowledge. This is a vital part of pastoral leadership because of the deeply personal connections and issues we deal with. They affect us emotionally and more personally, and managing our own sense of self within this can be crucial to our success.

Whilst this is a whistle-stop tour of leadership theory within pastoral care, the aim of this chapter is to highlight the importance of our own domain specific knowledge as pastoral leaders, and to help us know where to develop further as leaders. Too often, the genericism carries over into pastoral leaders, and we are left wondering how to be 'inspirational' when, in fact, we need to simply know more and more about our jobs and use this knowledge to make the best decisions about what to do when we face certain challenges.

Practical strategies

Leading and managing staff

This is something that often crops up in interview for pastoral roles: how will you manage a difficult form tutor? It can also be something that feels intimidating when you are new to the role, especially if you are less experienced in the classroom than the staff you lead. In managing difficult tutors, I often find it is learning about them and their motivations that helps to lead them more effectively. Find out what motivates them, what they enjoy, and what they're good at. Create opportunities for them to excel at this. It is also important to be clear with your form tutors about what you want them to be doing. They can't meet expectations if you aren't clear about what those expectations are. This can be as simple as ensuring that each day there is a bulletin reminding them of what you want them to do on a given morning. Following up and being a presence during these times is also important – you're able to notice if what you need to happen is happening. This shows both staff and students that you value their time and effort.

Of equal importance when leading and managing staff in pastoral roles, I think, is when our team can see what their role is in the bigger picture. Often, a lot the things they will be asked to do will be important in the grand scheme of keeping the wheels turning at an operational level, but sometimes we don't always communicate that with them. As professionals, we know we do important work, and it won't do any harm to be clear about that regularly with your team.

Difficult conversations

There will come a time, probably quite quickly in your career, where you find some members of your team are not meeting your expectations. You'll need to have one of the much dreaded, often hypothesised about difficult conversations.

Open and honest conversations if staff are not meeting your expectations are really, really important. No one likes having difficult conversations, but a problem is rarely solved by ignoring it. It helps, when approaching difficult conversations, to remember that kindness and compassion are fundamental to working with other human beings, and for me that comes from the understanding that no one comes to work and deliberately sets out to do a bad job. The purpose of any conversation such as this comes from finding out what the problem is and what barriers are preventing staff from doing what you need, and from working together to prevent it happening again. My top tips for this include:

- **Clarity.** You need to fully understand what the problem is and have the full facts. If you don't have these in full, your conversation should start with the staff member also contributing to this. This is especially the case where you might have information from students that may not reflect the reality. Your team need to know that you will give them the professional respect of finding out all the information needed rather than just some of it.
- **Your behaviour.** This can make or break a difficult conversation. Just as in the classroom you set the tone, the same is true of a

difficult conversation. Pay particular attention to your body language and your tone of voice.

- **Face to face.** If it's an important conversation, give it the importance it deserves and do it face to face. An email might seem easier, but it'll never be anywhere near as effective.

- **Language use.** It's important not to apportion blame or bring emotion into a conversation like this. Using phrases such as 'I noticed ...' to talk about the problem allows it to feel more neutral and less combative than 'You did ...'

- **Follow up.** If you've taken the time to talk about a problem, you also need to take the time to follow up on it, especially where things have been resolved well. This allows you time to refocus on the positives and offer praise and reassurance where things have become better. A thank you, or simply noticing, can go a long way to building excellent relationships with your team.

Owning your mistakes

First and foremost, it's important to acknowledge that you will make mistakes. You're human. We are fallible. If you're anything like me, you'll hate making mistakes. It is vital, however, that you take responsibility for them. They're your actions – you need to own them. Simple phrases, such as 'I'm sorry, I got that wrong' or 'This is on me – I have dropped the ball on this', work well. Simple phrases but powerful ones. As leaders, we have a responsibility to do this, whether it is to our line manager about something we have done wrong or to a form tutor or teacher where we have made a poor judgement. It can be tempting to try to save yourself and hide from mistakes, but this is going to do more damage. Teachers and school professionals, as well as students, are far more receptive to a genuine apology and responsibility for an error than we might think. This extends to parents too. Where we have genuinely got something wrong, we need to take responsibility openly. And then put it right.

Key Learning Points

- Pastoral leadership can become neglected when it comes to leadership development. We need to own our own development.

- We can become tied up in the 'hero model' of pastoral leadership. This is unhelpful.
- Great leadership, be that pastoral or otherwise, is based upon domain specific knowledge.
- Our leadership should improve with experience because this is where we gain the most expertise.
- Reflection is vital in our leadership journey.

Case study

Rowena has been head of year 8 for six weeks. A student arrives at her office door. She's never met them before. They are upset and tell her they are being bullied. Rowena hasn't dealt with bullying before, and she's not sure what to do next. She's not sure what to ask the student or how to deal with this conversation. The student leaves having not really told her what's going on.

Note down:

1. What would you do in this situation?
2. What knowledge do you have of similar situations and how would you deal with things differently?
3. What would your professional advice be to Rowena?
4. What should she do next?
5. What is it that she is lacking in at this stage to act as a guide for her practice?

RECOMMENDED READING

Lock, S. (ed.) (2020). *The researchED Guide to Leadership: An evidence-informed guide for teachers.* Woodbridge: John Catt Educational.

This chapter has touched upon some of the most important aspects of this book, but it is a much deeper treasure trove of knowledge of school leadership. There are chapters on all aspects of school leadership, from inclusion to curriculum leadership. Pastoral leaders, in my opinion, should be well read and engaged in the latest thinking around our leadership. This book is a thought-provoking and interesting delve into the argument that excellent leadership comes from excellent knowledge.

Evans, M. (2019). *Leaders with Substance: An antidote to leadership genericism in schools.* Woodbridge: John Catt Educational. This is a comprehensive delve into school leadership – a must read for any developing school leader.

REFERENCES

Barker, J. and Rees, T. (2020). Developing School Leadership. In Lock, S. (ed.) *The researchED Guide to Leadership: An evidence-informed guide for teachers.* Woodbridge: John Catt Educational.

Barker, J. and Rees, T. (2020). What is School Leadership? In Lock, S. (ed.) *The researchED Guide to Leadership: An evidence-informed guide for teachers.* Woodbridge: John Catt Educational.

Bereiter, C. and Scardamalia, M. (1993). *Surpassing ourselves: An inquiry into the nature and implications of expertise.* Chicago, IL: Open Court.

Bloom, B.S. (1984). The 2-sigma problem. The search for methods of group instruction as effective as one-to-one tutoring, *Educational Researcher,* 13, pp. 4–16.

Cardno, C. (2012). *Managing Effective Relationships in Education.* Los Angeles, CA: SAGE.

DuFour, R. and Marzano, R.J. (2011). *Leaders of Learning: How district, school and classroom leaders improve student achievement.* Bloomington, IN: Solution Tree Press.

Evans, M. (2019). *Leaders with Substance: An antidote to leadership genericism in schools.* Woodbridge: John Catt Educational.

Grove, M. (2004). The Three R's of Pastoral Care: Relationships, respect and responsibility, *Pastoral Care in Education,* 22, pp. 34–38.

Hallinger, P. and Heck, R.H. (2011). Conceptual and Methodological Issues in Studying School Leadership Effects as a Reciprocal Process, *School Effectiveness and School Improvement,* 22, pp. 149–173.

Hayes, D., Christie, P., Mills, M. and Lingard, B. (2004). Productive leaders and productive leadership: Schools as learning organisations,

Journal of Educational Administration, 42(5), pp. 520–538. https://doi.org/10.1108/09578230410554043.

Kahneman, D. and Klein, G. (2009). Conditions for Intuitive Expertise: A failure to disagree, *American Psychologist*, 64, pp. 515–526.

Kennedy, M. (2016). How Does Professional Development Improve Teaching? *Review of Education Research*, 86, pp. 945–980.

Leithwood, K. (2007). The Emotional Side of School Improvement: A leadership perspective. In T. Townsend (ed.) *The International Handbook on School Effectiveness and Improvement* (pp. 615–634). Dordrecht: Springer.

Leithwood, K., Anderson, S., Mascall, B. and Straus, T. (2010). School Leaders' Influences on Student Learning: The four paths. In T. Bush, L. Bell and D. Middlewood (eds.) *The Principles of Educational Leadership and Management*. London: Sage.

Lock, S. (ed.) (2020). *The researchED Guide to Leadership: An evidence-informed guide for teachers*. Woodbridge: John Catt Educational.

Louis, K.S., Dretzke, B. and Wahlstrom, K. (2010). How does Leadership Affect Student Achievement? Results from a national US survey, *School Effectiveness and School Improvement*, 21, pp. 315–336.

Purdy, N. (2013). Introduction. In N. Purdy (ed.) *Pastoral Care 11–16: A critical introduction* (pp. 1–8). London: Bloomsbury Academic.

Simon, H.A. (1992). What is an "explanation" of behaviour? *Psychological Science*, 3, pp. 150–161.

Tamati, A. (2011). Te Mana tangata – Leadership Stories, *Journal of Educational Leadership, Policy and Practice*, 26, pp. 69–74.

CHAPTER 8
SURVIVING AND THRIVING AS A PASTORAL LEADER

Our roles in school are crucial to the effective running of a school, but also in supporting students to achieve their very best. That said, it is undeniable that we have one of the most demanding roles in school. To say that we spin all the plates would be a wild underestimation of our daily lives. It is a frantic, demanding, fast-paced role – one that it is hard to truly understand unless you have done the job.

Lots of people say that teaching is an unpredictable job – pastoral care makes it look like a delightfully stable job! The reality is that we can go from one extreme to the other within seconds.

The truth is that emotionally demanding and sadly often harrowing cases can walk into our offices at any point. When I reflect on those moments in my own career, I've gone from life-changing, devastating scenarios with young people straight into teaching Shakespeare to year 10 within seconds. Our brains adapt to the role, and we learn coping mechanisms, but the reality of our roles is that they are difficult. That word doesn't seem to rightly capture the essence of what we do, but it's true, nonetheless. This frenetic, traumatic working life we lead is extremely demanding to navigate.

I wanted to include a chapter on this because it's vital. So much of our work is unseen – our colleagues have little idea about what we do all day. They rarely learn about the distressing, harrowing moments we face alongside our young people. And the truth is, this takes a toll on you. It's very easy to say we should be detached and not take the stresses of the job home. I'd argue that's impossible. The young people we have the privilege of working with are wonderful. They're human beings. We see the very best and the very worst moments in their lives. We care deeply about them, not just on the surface, but we often know them so well, and spend so much time supporting them, that it's incredibly difficult not to feel a small emotional connection. We would not be human if we did not feel compassion and care for them.

Of course, we keep a professional distance, and endeavour not to become 'too involved', but the reality is that we do become invested in their lives, because we care. It can be hard to manage, especially alongside all the other demands on our time.

In this chapter, I wanted to devote time and words to what I've learnt over my time in pastoral care and hopefully share some insights into how to manage this. This chapter is a little different from the others. It doesn't feature research and evidence. It's purely a chapter devoted to the common issues that we deal with regularly, and some things I have learnt over my career that I hope will bring either some new ideas or a familiar sense of relief that we all face similar battles, day in and day out. You'll have many other experiences that aren't covered – the thing about pastoral care is that we all bring our own experiences to it. Different issues will affect us differently. But I hope to explore some of the ways that this role can be kept manageable and not consume you entirely. In saying that, I'm sure I've portrayed an awful view of the role. That isn't how I feel. I genuinely believe that this is the very best role in a school. It is a joy, an honour, and a privilege; we are lucky to have such an incredible job where we do genuinely change lives.

Pastoral provision

This is one of the core aspects of what we do – we run the provision and experiences for often huge year groups or key stages. It's a huge undertaking – an extra teaching and learning responsibility, if you will. Schools all have different models of pastoral care, registration, and time allocated, but on average, I would suggest that there is at least an hour, if not more, of time each week that we need to resource and prepare.

When I first went into pastoral care, a lot of what I did was relatively unplanned. It was a case of 'What can I do with them this week?' It took me a while to realise that this approach was somewhat backwards. There was little thought and time being invested – and this ended up wasting a lot of student time. Frantic searches on the *Times Educational Supplement* (TES) resources and pastoral websites often gave me a time filler, but it had little relevance or development in the grand scheme of things. Over time, I realised that this time needed to be more explicitly planned for. I realised that pastoral provision needed as much investment as the academic curriculum.

But time is scarce in our professional lives. I needed to take a different approach. What I began doing was to think about my provision over a prolonged period of time – a term. What could be achieved over this time? What were our students' emerging needs? I spent some time thinking about what wider knowledge and opportunities would most benefit our cohort, and loosely divided it into:

- General knowledge and cultural capital
- Literacy and reading
- Study skills and learning
- Character development

From this, I devoted a day a week to each of these loose themes. Rather than plan and resource these weekly, I took a more front-loaded approach, and put together resources for the whole term. This was most easily done through the production of booklets – it meant I could do the work up front, have the booklets copied in advance, and a term's worth of provision was ready. It required a good chunk of time up front, but this freed me up entirely during the working week to not have to think about this – it was all done in advance, and easy for form tutors to deliver. It made managing my own workload easier, as it did for form tutors too.

In truth, it was more of a curriculum leader approach, but I do believe strongly that we have a role to play in this too. The time we have with students can be used in powerful ways and contribute to the development of our young people. From talking about current events, to reading extracts from classic texts, to learning about learning, a wide, varied, but relevant provision can be created. This gives purpose to registration time.

Of course, as we know all too well, there are times when you need to be more reactive as a pastoral leader. I made sure that the programme of study could be easily paused to make room for a more urgent need. For example, if there are particular issues within your school, or in your local community, or in the wider world, it is only right that you give these the time they need. Be flexible, but be prepared.

It's the best thing I ever did and, of course, once materials are put together, they can be used again in future – it's a workload friendly approach that really helped me keep my head above water.

Day-to-day life

One of the hardest parts of our role is how unpredictable it is. I learnt very early on never to plan to get something done in a day – it is the unwritten rule in pastoral care that when you desperately need to get some exams marked, a serious incident will occur and will drain any time and energy you had ready to do your marking. Balancing this, and balancing your day, are crucial to your success as a pastoral leader. Without this balance, it is all too easy to become entirely overwhelmed with things coming your way, and a backlog is created within days.

Each morning, I spend ten minutes getting my head around all the 'little issues' I haven't managed to pick up the day before. By 'little issues', I mean those that are often resolved in a few minutes – a quick conversation here and there. These get added to my daily bulletin – tutors send these students on to me in morning registration, meaning that I can clear the desk of these promptly. I find this quicker than trying to do this later in the day when you inevitably end up walking a million miles around your school to locate students, only to discover they're in a music lesson, or their PE lesson is cross country!

Once I'm clear on the little things, I then schedule the bigger things. Each day, if you're a teaching head of year, your available time will be different – you're at the behest of your timetable. Free periods earlier on in the day are a gift from the timetable gods – use these to get ahead of yourself, and deal with the bigger things earlier in the day. Think of it as a race against time; you never know when something will come along and blow up!

Alongside this, when I'm scheduling my day, I try to ensure, especially on days where I have a little more time, that there is a protected period for proactive work. This is the first thing to go in a busy pastoral leader's life, but it is arguably one of the most important things. Protect it with your life. These proactive tasks, such as a pre-emptive attendance conversation or something you're working on to improve an aspect of your school, need to be given the time they rightly deserve. Of course, there will be days where a disclosure will come along and ruin your plans. That's fine – that's the nature of our job. But if it's a bunch of little things that could easily encroach on your proactive time, don't allow it to. Proactive work is where our best work is done – this allows us to get ahead of problems before they develop. Some days, it's merely ten minutes; other days, it might be longer. I try to make sure that I commit to three proactive things I will do each day. It might be a call to a parent, a conversation with another teacher – things that can really help in the long run.

As part of my proactive time, I also try to break up the larger things I might have on into smaller tasks done each day, so that I make progress towards them, rather than leaving them until the last minute when it is a dauntingly huge task.

I also make sure that when I am planning my day I make some time for visibility. This is one of the most powerful tools at your disposal. If students know you are an ever-present entity in their lives, this changes their behaviour and attitudes over time. I like to make sure I am visible in a morning as they enter school – this allows me to 'be seen looking'.

Primarily this is about standards. If students know you're on the door, checking their uniform, for example, they're more likely, in my experience at least, to self-regulate this and get themselves sorted with coats off, top buttons done up, etc. It's a small thing, but an incredibly important thing. I try to make sure I am also able to do the same at break and lunch. A lot of your lunch times as a pastoral leader end up taken with duties – try to work with your duty timetable to make sure your duties allow you to be a visible presence in your year group. You know these students inside out, you can read the room, test the atmosphere, and generally deal with things far more efficiently than someone who isn't in the position you are in. My workload might not always appreciate it, but I prefer being on duty every lunch time with my year group. In the long run, this actually saves me time. I can deal with a number of issues whilst out and about with students. The small but powerful conversations, the opportunities for praise, the opportunities for building relationships, and for crafting your standards, cannot be underestimated. This is your other opportunity to 'be seen looking' and to reinforce your standards and expectations.

Our days are always busy, but it's also incredibly important to make sure you have time to eat and drink properly. There's nothing worse than a hangry pastoral leader. It can be easy to neglect your own welfare in this job – you're so focussed on the welfare of others. There are days, though, where time is of the essence. I always make sure I have things like nutritionally sound meal replacement products that can be used in an emergency. The reality of our jobs is that sometimes we are going to struggle to find time to eat and drink properly, but finding strategies that work for you to make sure that you can is important. Also, make sure you have emergency chocolate on hand, mostly for you, but also helpful when a crying person lands at your door.

Marking and planning

Whilst this book has been written with both teaching and non-teaching pastoral leaders in mind, it would be remiss of me not to comment on the workload of classroom teaching. If you're not a teaching pastoral leader, skip this bit!

As an English teacher, with a predominately GCSE-based timetable, my workload from class teaching is a challenge. Planning, marking, and feedback are a huge part of the job. It's easy to neglect your teaching responsibilities alongside managing your pastoral role, but you need to avoid this at all costs. You are, first and foremost, a teacher. You have the education of students in your hands. This is important work we are doing.

Despite its importance, it's also, occasionally, an unwelcome distraction. It places a huge demand on your time which cannot be underestimated.

In much the same way that I approach pastoral provision, my planning takes a similar route. I plan on a half termly basis and have the essentials in place in advance. This means that all curriculum planning is resourced up front. Sometimes this is in a booklet form. Other times it may be a homework booklet. It very much depends on your whole school and departmental approach to curricular provision, but I cannot overestimate how important it is to do a lot of this work up front. After each lesson, I make a note of what I would need to do next lesson, tweaking my plans based on the emerging learning needs of students. This isn't a time intensive process, especially if you are an experienced classroom teacher. But this approach is crucial in helping me keep my head above water. It means that my planning and teaching are the very best they can be and remain relatively unaffected by my pastoral responsibilities.

In essence, my approach is that if it can be done ahead of time, do it. Automating homework tasks, for example, really helps me. I know that one task a week will be knowledge testing on a VLE – and these are pre-set over a half term to specific dates so that they go live at the right time for students. This is one less thing to think about each week, and one less thing that might, on busy weeks, fall to the bottom of my priority list.

Marking and feedback are a huge part of classroom teaching, especially at GCSE and A level. Where possible, making use of ICT and using self-marking quizzes online can be helpful. Not only does it save you time, but it's also an excellent use of students' learning time, giving them fast and effective feedback, but also giving you useful information about gaps in learning, illuminating your priorities for the classroom.

Exam time, however, presents pastoral leaders with huge challenges. It can add, for me at least as an English teacher, between ten and twelve hours' extra work a week. Looking ahead to when this is, I try to make sure I keep that week as free as it can be in terms of meetings or after-school commitments. Equally, I try to ensure that I devote time for this within my plan for the week. Rather than try to do this during the school day, which is often impossible as a busy pastoral leader, I schedule time for this after school. I also leave the office to get this done – or go into hiding, as I call it!

It may be that you work better at home or have family commitments. What works for one won't always work for another. But the one thing that is important is in planning your time and using what you know about your own self-regulation to do it. For example, I couldn't plan to mark at weekends, because I know myself well enough to know that all that will happen is that my marking will have a lovely adventure in the car, but ultimately not leave the car until I return to work on the Monday. We all have our own strengths and weaknesses – you need to work with yours rather than aimlessly hoping you'll do something you know is not realistic.

Emotional support

One of the biggest unseen demands of our role is on our emotional wellbeing. The issues we deal with are often distressing, heartbreaking things, and this can and does take its toll on us as people. It's important to acknowledge this and know that looking after ourselves as human beings is a vital part of the job – without it, we can't be at our best for those relying on us to be so.

One thing that does develop with time is the ability to compartmentalise the things we deal with. It's about finding ways to leave the emotional things at school. However, there isn't, in my experience at least, a simple solution to this. There will be some issues that stay with you, that you mull over as you're trying to sleep. I think it's important to acknowledge this and not to see it as a weakness. It's the human part of the job. But it can, sometimes, become more all-consuming than might be healthy.

It's helpful to have support networks around you because of this. Schools are, increasingly, making use of formal supervision for pastoral staff. If your school isn't yet making the most of this, it's a good opportunity to discuss it. It is a helpful use of time to talk through the most challenging issues that you face, and have the opportunity to reflect, refine, and improve what you're doing.

It's also important to have down time, away from work, where your focus is on something else. For some – OK me – this might be watching gloriously trashy TV on the weekend. For others, this will be getting out of the house, going for a walk, wild swimming – whatever you love doing. I try to see this as part of the job – we must look after ourselves so that we can look after others. It's like when you're on an aeroplane and they tell you to put your oxygen mask on before helping others, should the worst happen. We need to approach our lives in the same way. This means not letting your hobbies fall by the wayside. It means trying to eat well and exercise. It means looking after your own mental health. We can become so consumed with helping others that we inevitably feel guilty about helping ourselves. We need to fight this instinct and remember that we are human beings too. One question I often ask myself if I know I'm not quite looking after myself as I should is what advice I'd give myself were I my own head of year. I know the answer – I just have to do it!

My final tip on this, especially when it comes to days when you're feeling particularly glum about something, is to get yourself back amongst the kids. Go and speak to the kids who get it right day in, day out. Go and see them learning in a lesson. Go and watch them playing football at lunch time. Kids are wonderful, and being around them is a tonic. I guarantee that one of them will make you laugh, or bring you pride, within minutes, and remind you why you do the job you do. Kids are ace – spend time helping them see that.

Planning ahead

I've already written about the need to plan ahead in terms of classroom responsibilities and pastoral provision, but there are other aspects of looking ahead and being organised that really help.

I have a confession here – I am not a naturally organised person. In fact, I'd go so far as to say I'm inherently disorganised and occasionally hectic. I have to work hard at being organised. And yet, organisation is one of the top skills we need as pastoral leaders. If you're someone who is naturally organised to within an inch of your life, congratulations. I'm jealous. If, however, like me, you need to work a bit harder at it, these are the things I have learnt about trying to be organised.

Your diary is your best friend. I use my Outlook calendar on my email and on my phone. I diarise everything, from my lessons, to meetings, to incremental deadlines. I use these as reminders, to hold myself accountable. If, for example, I have an Early Help meeting scheduled, a week before I will place a reminder in the diary to remind myself that I need to focus on preparation for this. I'll then add some time into my diary afterwards for the admin following on from the meeting. It may seem somewhat anal, but if I don't plan my work life like this, the wheels quickly fall off. We have so many competing demands that we need to play an assertive role in managing them equally so that we get them done to the best of our ability.

I also make sure that the school calendar is within my own calendar. I find this particularly helpful for scheduling meetings or phone calls with parents. If, for example, I know that in one week I have INSET until 5, and a GCSE assessment to mark, I will try to keep that week free from anything else. But I must make sure that I have these in the diary in the first place to try to avoid having the week from hell. Sometimes, you don't have that flexibility, but where I can, I will.

Record-keeping is also a key part of being organised as a pastoral leader. I ensure that the last thing I do each day before leaving school is to record all the things I need to record. It may be inputting an incident on your school safeguarding software. It may be recording notes from a phone call and filing them away. It may be a follow-up email. Some days there are lots, and these are the kinds of things that easily get missed in our busy lives. Making time for this each day may seem like hard work, but the records we keep are incredibly important. You never know when you might need them, so make sure that you've got everything you need. It doesn't always feel it at the time; in fact, it feels like a bit of a pain. But I cannot stress how important this is.

Professional development

Professional development as a pastoral leader is something that is often neglected, both in terms of in-school provision and within your own time. One thing that's clear from this book is that we are incredibly busy, and dedicating time to our own development is yet another area that can all too easily fall by the wayside as we have the demands of sometimes just getting through the day in one piece. And yet, it is a vital use of our time. We owe it to those we care for to ensure that we are the very best professionals we can be for them.

To make sure that this is kept on my radar, I schedule some protected time, at least once a half term, when I will invest in my own development.

There are a few areas I have found incredibly useful in this. The first is through the National Association for Pastoral Care in Education (NAPCE), a professional agency for those who have an active interest in pastoral care. Their role is in supporting and informing pastoral workers, but also in disseminating good practice, alongside promoting education, training, and development opportunities. Their journal is one of the few areas of research that focusses on our area of responsibility. It's an excellent body where I have read countless important pieces of work that have developed me as a professional.

I also regularly dip in and out of educational publications such as the *Times Educational Supplement* (TES) and *Teach Secondary*, both of which often have interesting publications relevant to us as professionals. I tend to use an app on my phone to store these up, where I see them even if I don't have time to fully read and digest them just then. By keeping them in one place, I can dip in and out of things when I do have time to dedicate to my own development.

Further to this, immersing yourself in professional reading is important. I believe that it is our professional responsibility to be as informed as we can be about all aspects of education, because this inevitably crosses over into pastoral care in one way, shape, or form. I regularly read books about teaching and learning, leadership, and whole school management. Whilst they're clearly not primarily aimed at pastoral care, the content nevertheless will be relevant in some ways. If I hadn't done this, I wouldn't, for example, be in the position that I am in to best educate our students about how best to learn and to study.

Conferences can also be useful to us, again giving us new insights or direction towards things that are useful or important to what we do; researchED, for example, run conferences focussed on what the evidence tells us about education. I have learnt so much from every researchED conference I've been to. For example, this is where I first learnt about a crucial study, hardly known in the real world of schools, into the best ways of teaching at-risk children – Project Follow Through. The work of Zig Engelmann, the leading researcher on the project, is transformational, and gives us incredibly important insights into how best to teach disadvantaged students, and how best they learn. If you haven't come across it yet, it's a must read, not just for its somewhat questionable title!

Whilst this might, on the surface at least, be concerned with teaching and learning, I believe it is imperative that we are just as well informed on issues pertaining to our students' learning as academic middle and senior leaders are. We are, after all, all aiming for the same thing – the very best learning outcomes for our students.

Key Learning Points
- Our role is physically and emotionally challenging.
- We must look after our own wellbeing.
- Pre-planning and resourcing can help you free up time in your working week.
- Proactive pastoral care is an important part of our work, and we must protect the time we need to do this.
- Organisation is crucial, and you need to find techniques that work for you.
- Record-keeping must remain high on the priority list.

RECOMMENDED READING

Lane, S. (2020). *Beyond Wiping Noses: Building an informed approach to pastoral leadership in schools.* Williston, VT: Crown House Publishing.

This is an excellent book about evidence informed pastoral care. I would fully recommend this as a professional development text, but also one from which you will learn a lot about thriving as a pastoral leader.

REFERENCES

Lane, S. (2020). *Beyond Wiping Noses: Building an informed approach to pastoral leadership in schools.* Williston, VT: Crown House Publishing.

CHAPTER 9
COMMON PASTORAL PROBLEMS

One of the most interesting aspects of our roles is the wide variety of issues that we deal with. It is never a boring job, and you never know what's going to come your way.

Regardless of what does come your way, there's rarely a set response to how you will deal with it. Context really is king when it comes to pastoral care. Even where you might follow a set process, the way in which you approach it and the pitch of your conversations all very much depend on the child and on the family. Although this is very much one of the appeals of the job, there are some common problems that underpin what we do. I wanted to devote some time to this, and to share some advice and guidance that I've had over the years. Your implementation of this should, of course, be guided by your context, but I do think that one thing that's often missing from the wider conversations in pastoral care is how we deal with the same issues, the ones that are common occurrences. Sharing good practice can be revolutionary, and a lot of what I will explore in this chapter is based on years of learning from others.

Self-harm

This is something that I would say I deal with increasingly. Whether this is in response to the pressures of the COVID-19 pandemic, or simply because of the increased support around talking about mental health, I don't know. What I do know is that it is something that every pastoral leader will deal with at least on a semi regular basis. Recent statistics, as outlined by Mental Health First Aid (MHFA) England (2020), suggest just how common it is. They state that about 18% of students aged 12–17 report having self-harmed at some point in their life, and this is 2–3 times more common in female students. On average, their research suggests self-harming commonly begins between age 13 and age 15, although it is important to remember that it can happen at any age. They also outline that students who identify as LGBTQ+ are more likely to report self-harming than are young people who do not identify as LGBTQ+. This just goes to show how common it is, and that this is something you will deal with as a pastoral leader very frequently.

It's never a nice issue to deal with – a child is hurting emotionally and expressing that physically. It's a real privilege of the job that students disclose personal things like this and make themselves potentially more vulnerable. It means they trust us, and feel that they can open up, and this can only ever be a good thing. In an ideal world, we wouldn't get to this point, but it happens, and it is frequent, in my experience.

One of the best CPD opportunities I've had in recent years, and one which really helps when dealing with disclosures such as this, is the Youth Mental Health First Aid training. The central focus of the training is around the way we respond when young people talk to us about their mental health difficulties. Their training shows the importance of simply listening, reassuring, and responding. These are three key verbs to reassure ourselves with. I often think it is in our nature as pastoral leaders to want to fix things immediately, and make things better for young people, and you can feel under pressure from yourself to have all the answers. This is rarely helpful in cases such as this. One of the key parts of the training focussed on what young people tell us about what actually helps in situations such as this, and the overwhelming majority talked about the most important one – listening.

Simply letting the child talk, openly and without judgement, is key in instances like this. Reassure them that they've done the right thing in talking to you and that you are there to support them. Respond to what they're saying, but don't go in hard with questions or talk about yourself – simply gesturing and encouraging them to keep talking is enough. They need to know they are being heard rather than simply being listened to.

I tend to have a mental checklist in situations like this, and ensure that my immediate response is to always listen, reassure, and respond. One of the things you do need to gain from the conversation is around the level of risk – this dictates a lot of your next steps. If a child's life or health is in immediate danger – for example, if their self-harm has been an overdose – then emergency action must be taken in the form of calling 999. This is why it's important to listen, but also to make sure that the conversation is guided to cover the important things you need to know to keep them safe.

If their health and life are not in immediate danger, it's still important to find out more about how the child is feeling. My mental checklist to ensure that the conversation covers the important things is:

- Who knows about their self-harm? Do parents? What about friends?
- What have they used to harm themselves with?
- Is there any support in place already?
- Has the child been to a GP about their mental health?
- Have they thought about harming themselves again? Do they plan to?
- Are they feeling suicidal?
- Do they have a plan for suicide?

The last two are particularly important, but they can feel like huge questions to ask a child. One thing I have learnt is that they are questions we shouldn't feel embarrassed or scared to ask. Asking the question won't make them more likely to be suicidal. It will, however, help you keep them safe. The first few times I asked a child this, I felt worried about doing it. In time, I learnt I had nothing to worry about. Talking openly about suicide can be difficult, but it's vital in keeping our children safe.

Over time, it's also important, if you don't already know, to find out more about the child's life and context. There may well be stresses and pressures we are unaware of that will come out in their own time, and this is why long-term support is so important. It can take some students a while to open up about other things in their lives, and it takes a while to build up trust. Keeping the conversation open, checking in with the child, and making time for them to talk are key here to getting the right support in place over time. This might be a GP appointment, a school counsellor, a mental health worker, an external agency; context, as I outlined earlier, is key.

It's also important, when dealing with self-harm, to recognise that it may take many forms. One often overlooked behaviour is more frequently displayed in male students. This often takes the form of punching things – walls, lockers, etc. What can display as aggressive behaviour should always be looked at through the lens of what it is – a deliberate behaviour designed to inflict harm on themselves. Self-harm is often stereotypically viewed as cutting, but it does take many forms, from hitting and punching things, to excessive drinking, drug-taking, or burning.

Bullying

Although schools have put a lot of effort and resources into improving their policy on bullying, and creating school environments where bullying is rare, it would be naïve to believe it doesn't happen. It can happen anywhere, no matter how well you might feel your school has created a culture where it doesn't.

The DfE (2017) define bullying as 'behaviour by an individual or group, usually repeated over time, which intentionally hurts another individual or group either physically or emotionally'. Repeated acts of behaviour like this can have a substantial impact on our young people, and it often leads to a decrease in their emotional and physical wellbeing. It's something that everyone who works with children must take seriously. All schools are required, by law, to have an anti-bullying policy that clearly explains what a school's response to bullying will be. It's vital that you know your own policy inside out because this is something that you will, unfortunately, likely deal with.

Bullying can take different forms: physical, verbal, or emotional. It can also happen online, which we have come to understand as cyber bullying. With the increasing social use of smartphones, social media is often at least part of most bullying incidents that I have dealt with. It's important to remember that this means there is rarely an escape for the victim – where once bullying may have happened solely in school, it now takes place in bedrooms and living rooms across the country. It can be easy to say to students 'Just turn it off', but it is rarely that simple or that easy for them. Social media plays a huge role in their lives, and we do need to acknowledge that, whether we agree with them using it or not!

We are often well placed to notice the signs of bullying in our young people, as are our pastoral staff such as form tutors, as well as class teachers. We spend a lot of time with our young people, and we get to know them incredibly well. This means that when something isn't quite right, we need to listen to our gut instinct. Some signs that a child might be bullied could be (Cumbria Safeguarding Children's Board 2021):

- Being frightened or reluctant to come to school, or about their journey to or from school
- Feeling ill in mornings
- Attendance declines or truancy
- Declining academic performance
- Having their belongings such as books destroyed or damaged
- Becoming withdrawn, lacking confidence, being distressed or anxious
- Eating problems
- Self-harm
- Suicidal ideation or intent
- Missing possessions
- Needing money having 'lost' it, or beginning to steal things from others
- Reluctance to talk about what's wrong
- Unexplained injuries
- Changes in behaviour, such as aggression or disengaged behaviour, or bullying behaviours towards siblings

This is by no means an exhaustive list, and the impact of bullying can be seen in a myriad of behaviours, but it is something that we must ensure that we are attuned to, and that our staff are too. Encouraging your team and those that teach your year group to trust their gut instinct is fundamental. In my experience, teachers can sometimes feel like they're wasting your time if it feels like something small to them. It is vital that all your interactions with colleagues reassure them that this is not the case.

I often say that I'd rather hear about 20 things that are nothing than miss a child in distress or danger. It's an important message that can easily get lost in busy school lives, but you need to ensure that you really reflect this value in all that you do.

Once you become aware of a bullying issue, what you do next really matters. Bullying must never be tolerated or ignored in the hope that it will go away. A lot of your actions, as I've previously explored, will rely entirely on context. It's one of those scenarios where working with the child is really important. It takes time to build trust, and I always try to ensure that the child has an active and important role in the steps we take. They need to feel involved and listened to. It's a process you go through together. Bullying often feels unpredictable and the child is likely to feel hyper alert – acknowledging this and making sure there are no surprises in the things you do next is important to supporting them through this.

As with most things that we do as pastoral leaders, there must be a safeguarding consideration when dealing with incidents such as this. Behaviours such as physical or sexual violence are particular signs that there is a safeguarding need, and bullying incidents should always be something that you talk about with your designated safeguarding lead (DSL). It's also important to have similar conversations about the child who is displaying bullying behaviours. These can sometimes be an indication that you should have safeguarding concerns about them too, and this is an important part of the process that should not be overlooked.

Taking bullying seriously and acting upon any reports of it must be a priority in school. The child also needs to know they have your support in dealing with it. That said, it is something that is rarely straightforward. Of utmost importance is the regular review of the plans you have in place for the child. Things can change very quickly, and the child needs to know that they have a clear route for support. They can often feel as though telling an adult will make things worse, and you need to build up their trust by continuing to take their experiences seriously whilst also allowing them to feel in control of the process.

As part of your processes, it's vital, as with most things we do, that you have clear records kept; this means every phone call, every conversation, any action that you take.

Girls' friendships

Any experienced pastoral leader will tell you that girls' friendships and their falling out are one of the most frustrating things you can deal with. At times, it feels endless and as though it's taking over your entire professional life. Girls' friendships, and the intricate dynamics of them, are complex. When there is a breakdown in these relationships, all hell can break loose! Despite its challenges, there are some key things that I have, over time, found work well when trying to navigate a path through the carnage.

Boundary setting

Every student involved needs to know what the boundaries are – and the clearer, the better. For example, one of the things that often happens is girls 'looking at' one another, which can, on the surface, seem ludicrous. Having been a teenage girl, I can safely assure you that this is, in fact, an actual thing. It's akin to firing the first shot in a war. It is snide and sly, but it is also calculated and deliberate; its intention is to continue the battle between them. I have found spelling out these behaviours and making them known as 'red lines' is important in the solution. The same can be said of social media – there is an insidious way to use social media that looks like nothing at all to the untrained eye, but again can become another shot fired in the great friendship war. Rather than saying something like 'No unkind behaviours on social media', I tend to find something clearer, such as a mutual blocking of one another, allows you to be more precise with those involved. Which leads me on to the next thing …

Accountability

Any student involved in a fractious falling out needs to be held accountable for their own behaviour and the choices they make. Use the boundaries you set for those and make them as clear as they can be. Any grey area can be open to interpretation or abuse – your boundaries need to be clear to help you hold the students accountable for their own actions. For example, blocking on social media is very easy to hold them accountable for, whereas 'No unpleasant messages' can be very open to abuse, let's put it that way!

Communication

The way you communicate with those involved is important. This is also one of the reasons why issues like this take up an infinite amount of your time as a pastoral leader. In general, my golden rule is speaking to those involved on a 1:1 basis, but also as a group. Inevitably, they all tell each other what you've said when you're having a 1:1 conversation, but it's also important to do this with a group as a whole. It puts you in control of the messages that those involved take away and prevents any 'Well s/he said different to me', which girls can be masters at!

Navigating your way through these dynamics as a pastoral leader is also fraught with potential issues. In my experience, both sides of the argument will try to 'have you' on 'their side' and will use this to their advantage. You need to be incredibly careful not to say anything that may be perceived in this way and ensure that you are treating both sides equally. It's also important to openly talk about this with those involved and make it very clear that your role is not to get involved or take sides. You're the unbiased leader of the problem.

General agreements

One thing I always make sure to include in these processes is a clear agreement about conduct. I make sure that these are also shared with parents, who will, inevitably, also become embroiled in the issue. Everyone needs to be absolutely clear about what has been agreed, and acknowledging this with all students involved, and having them together when you do this, is a significant part of trying to move forward in a more positive way.

Do make sure you keep clear records of all that you do in situations like this – it can become increasingly complex, and fast-paced changes often happen literally overnight. Keeping these records helps you to keep yourself fully informed and in the best position to make decisions. It may also feel like it will last forever – it won't. At some point, some magical, mystic thing seems to happen, and it is rarely anything you will do. They'll suddenly become friends again, and it's like the whole thing never happened! Try to remember it won't last forever.

Problems with a teacher

This happens frustratingly frequently. A student, or a group of students, lands outside your office claiming 'He hates me' or some such other dramatic re-enactment of a problem. Students then indulge you with a dramatic retelling of the event.

It's easy, at this point, to think that they have indeed been mistreated. It's also important at this point to remember you're hearing one side of a story. This is especially important if you're a non-teaching pastoral leader. Not having that 'hands on' experience in the classroom can really bias the way in which you might view incidents like this.

Initially, when dealing with something like this, I tend to let the students talk, but I say little. It's likely, at this point, that they're looking to get you 'on side' – avoid this at all costs. You do, of course, have a duty to take their worries seriously and investigate them. At this point, I explain to them that I also need to speak to their teacher before we go forward with anything. I also find it useful to ask when their next lesson is so that I can try to deal with it quickly to prevent any further disruption to their learning, and to the teacher's teaching.

The way that you approach this with their teacher is essential. It's not professionally supportive to approach this as though they have done anything wrong – you don't know that for certain. You need to approach this in a way that shows you are supportive of the teacher – that really matters in situations such as this. Your language use also matters – I tend to actively avoid phrases such as 'your side' when talking about things like this. It's a small thing, but it shows that you're supporting the member of staff in finding out what has actually happened. Instead, I tend to use phrases such as 'Do you mind talking me through what happened?', which are void of any form of linguistic bias.

Quite often, you find a somewhat different explanation of events. Teachers don't go out of their way to cause issues with students; they certainly don't actively dislike students; nor do they go out of their way to make this clear whilst simultaneously destroying their own lesson. It's just not in their nature. It's often easy to see where the problem has arisen, and most teachers have the self-reflective abilities to see if they've got something wrong. And that's what we do need to remember; we are all human beings. We are fallible. We are working with other human beings, and we will all get things wrong from time to time. I can remember moments from my own classroom where I've totally misjudged a situation or said something that has inadvertently caused a problem. It happens. There's very little to be gained from the blame game here – your focus as a pastoral leader is to work with the teacher and the student to find a way forward. This is best done, in my experience, by sitting down with them together, with your role as the facilitator of the conversation. It is worth agreeing with the teacher beforehand what you both want the outcome to be, and to reassure them that your role is about helping that to happen, not to sit and be on the side of the student. There's very little to be gained in that sense, but it is important too to ensure that the child has the opportunity to be heard and to explain to their teacher what has been the problem or caused upset from their point of view. Open and honest conversation is best, with the focus keenly on moving beyond the problem and finding a solution together.

Refusal to attend school

This is one that you will come across from time to time, and there will always be a significant context. It is rare for a child to refuse to come to school if everything is genuinely fine. Your role here is primarily focussed on two things: getting them into the building and finding out what the problem is. One can be easier than the other, and this will be different with every child.

I find that meeting with the family and the child face to face is a helpful way to start this process; this is rarely the kind of issue that can be dealt with over the phone. In extreme circumstances, this may mean a home visit if you really cannot get the child to agree to come into the school to meet.

This first meeting needs to feel low threat to the child – things like not needing to wear uniform as they're only coming in to meet with you can help shape their perception of coming in. Finding a venue that feels less official can also help the child and their parents feel as though they can attend.

When you meet, give the family and the child some time to talk. In the past, I have made the mistake of jumping in too quickly with the focus on returning to school, and this has backfired. It's more important that they feel you are listening and care about what the problem is – and the purpose of this meeting is just that, finding out the barrier so that you can work with them to remove it.

There will be many potential barriers – friendship issues, a problem in a lesson, mental health, to name but a few. Your response will be very much based on context and on what is important with that individual child.

Essentially, your work here is in planning as low threat a return to school as possible. In my school, this often looks like making use of safe spaces such as an inclusion centre, where well-trained and compassionate staff will support the student if they are not ready to return to lessons. Plan out their day so they know what to expect – and, crucially, get their input into what they can manage.

There is little point in a plan which the child already feels is unrealistic. You'll be back to square one quickly. It's important to stress that this is a team effort – the parent has a role, the child has a role, and you have a role. I always ensure that everyone is clear on what they must do. For example:

- The parent will drive the child in to school.
- The child will come into the inclusion centre.
- I will arrange for some work to be there for them to do.

You would also then make sure your role focusses on the barrier the child is facing. It's also important that the child understands the importance of attending school. In some cases, talking them through the legal implications for their parents can help them see that they need to give it their all. For others, it can be linked to their academic success and the aspirations they have. Again, this will entirely depend on your knowledge of the child and their context. Regardless, it's important that all students know that getting an education is vital – it's something we all want for them.

Getting the right support in place for the child over the long term is also important. Your short-term goal is in getting them into school, but in the long term they may well need further support, especially if their school refusal is linked to mental health conditions that may come out as you work with the family. Finding coping strategies that work for the child will be an area that will need focus. This might be in the form of external resources such as national text lines like Young Minds, which allow them to access support 24/7 online. It might be that you need to explore involving other agencies and opening an Early Help to bring together other agencies that can help support the child. Regardless, it's important that support doesn't just stop as soon as they get back in – that support needs to be in place until the barriers to their attendance are fully removed.

Whilst these examples give you a taste of the things you will encounter regularly in your pastoral work, there will, of course, be many, many others. They will, I can guarantee, be lively and varied. They will challenge you as a pastoral leader, and as a person. They might well frustrate you. They'll sadden you often too. You never know what you'll be dealing with on any given day or time; this unpredictability is one of the things that I love most about the job. Even on days where I might be run ragged, the feeling of managing it all and making a difference to a child's life is humbling. Whatever issue you deal with, remember that there is a human being at the centre of it, usually one experiencing a difficulty or who may be in a very vulnerable place. As long as you always have their interests at heart, and you lead with that in mind, you won't go far wrong. You'll make mistakes; that really is part of the job. But if your intentions are good, and you make your decisions with that child's welfare in mind, you'll go far.

REFERENCES

Cumbria Safeguarding Children Partnership. (2021). *Bullying* [online]. Available from: www.cumbriasafeguardingchildren.co.uk. Accessed 23 August 2021.

Department for Education. (2017). *Preventing and Tackling Bullying* [online]. Available from: www.gov.uk. Accessed 23 August 2021.

ACKNOWLEDGEMENTS

I've learnt a lot over the course of writing this book, mostly about myself and what a nightmare I can be! I'm very lucky to be surrounded, in my life and in my career, by some incredible people that have supported me along the way, either with the book, or in the formative years of my career.

To Ian Routledge, who saw the potential in me when I didn't see it myself – and continues to do so to this day. I owe you a huge amount of gratitude and I feel privileged to work alongside you.

To Hugh Carter, for getting me hooked on this job 10 years ago and for teaching me to do it well.

To Jodie Sykes, the best head of year I've had the pleasure of working with – you gave me the confidence to start this book. You've taught me so much about this job. Proudly holding the line together, and being a bold, fierce, all-female Key Stage 4 team was a privilege and an honour. I hope we can recreate it in the future.

To Gill Todhunter, for forever being a constant source of wisdom, guidance, and the occasional rant. The impact you had during your 20 years in our school has changed so many lives – staff and students alike.

To the English department at my school, who are constantly a source of humour and fun. Thank you for putting up with me. Your hard work and dedication to our young people make me so very proud. Especially, thank you to Jen Hawley-McGee for being my forever work bestie.

To the very wonderful Ann Mroz MBE, Jon Severs, and Grainne Hallahan at the *Times Educational Supplement.* Thank you for getting me hooked on this writing thing – and for taking a chance on me. The work you do is a proud part of our profession and long may it continue.

To my friends Emma-Cate Stokes and Shannen Doherty, who have supported me every step of the way, listened to endless wittering voice notes, and been my cheerleaders when I needed you.

To Abby Deeks and Melissa Relph for their endless geekery and love of all things teaching, schools, and education. Where would I be without you two geeks?

I couldn't have done any of this without the support of my family. To Emma Clucas, my cousin and my best friend, and the best physics teacher colleague in the world. Some people warn against working with your family – they're wrong. Thank you for being in my life. You are one of the strongest people I know.

And, finally, to Mum and Dad, who taught me the value of hard work. Thank you for your endless love and support; I wouldn't be where I am today without you. I hope I can continue to make you proud every day – love Bundle x.